Grand Diplôme Cooking Course

A Danbury Press Book

The Danbury Press

a division of Grolier Enterprises, Inc.

Robert B. Clarke Publisher

This book has been adapted from the Grand Diplôme Cooking Course, originally published by Purnell Cookery, U.S.A.

Library of Congress Catalog Card Number: 72-13896

Filmsetting by Petty and Sons Ltd., Leeds, England.
Printed in the United States of America

1234567899876543

All recipes have been tested either at the Cordon Bleu Cookery School in London or in our U.S. test kitchens.

Note: all recipe quantities in this book serve 4 people unless otherwise stated.

Contents

MENUS

FEATURES

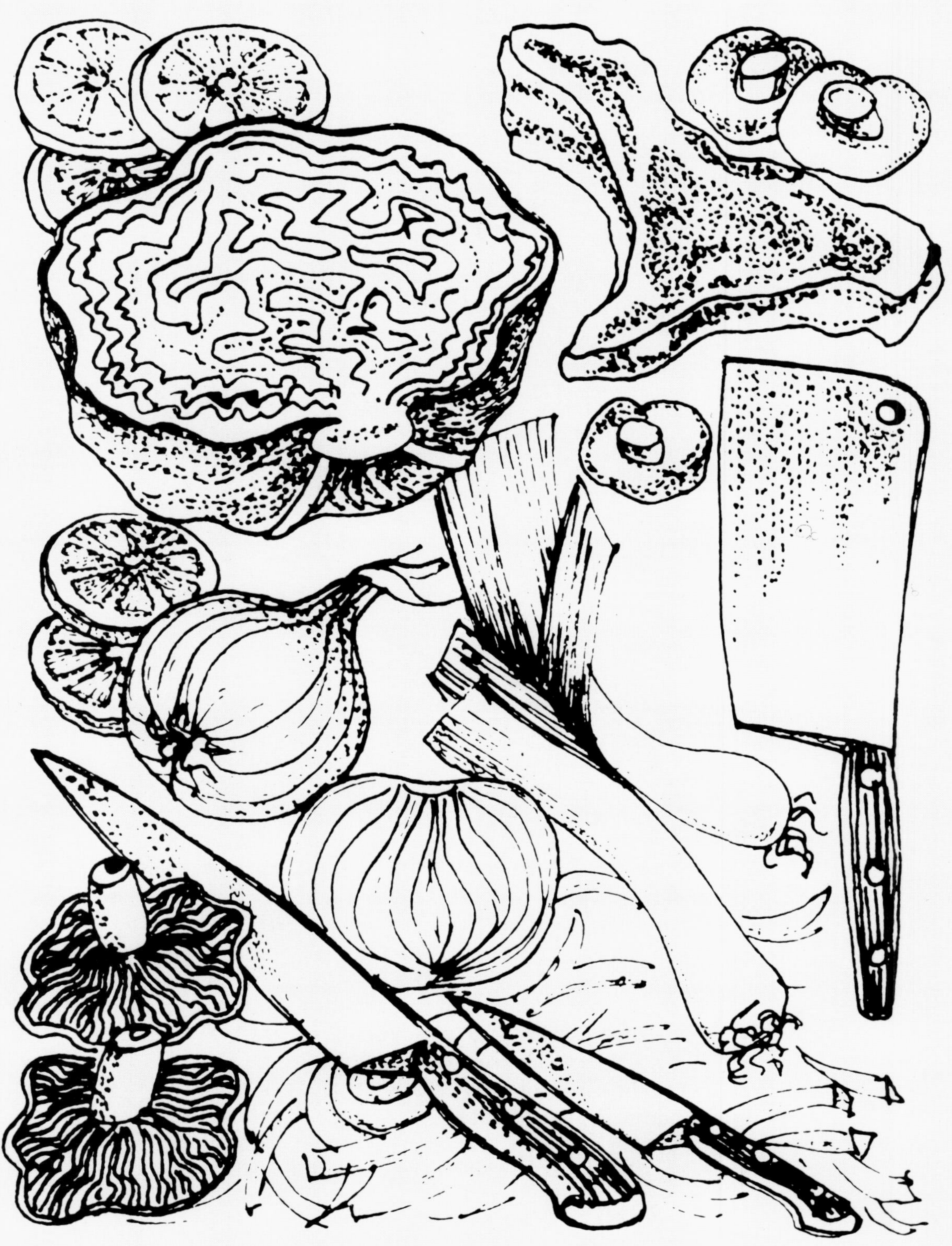

From the Editor

The perfect soufflé is the novice cook's ambition and the pride of the accomplished chef. In Volume 10 of your Grand Diplôme Cooking Course, you'll find light-as-air **Soufflés** made easy with the techniques taught at the Cordon Bleu Cookery School in London. Start with a simple soufflé omelet or a roulade flavored with salmon, then turn to the delights of curry-spiced crab soufflé, or the famous soufflé Grand Marnier.

Equally French is the art of **Cooking with Wine**. Wine is one of the easiest ways to add richness to sauces and succulence to meats, and many of the combinations, like beef with Burgundy and ham with Madeira, are classics. Wine is also wonderful with **Shellfish**; in this second lesson on shellfish – lobsters, oysters, mussels and shrimps star in recipes like oysters Rockefeller, flavored with Pernod, and magnificent lobster thermidor served in the shell with a sauce of white wine, heavy cream, tarragon and Parmesan cheese.

In more economical vein are some **Cold-weather Dishes** – hearty favorites like boiled beef with dumplings and Brunswick stew. But if stew seems too much like the old routine, try out some of the flamboyant foods of **Central Europe** – fish in black sauce, duck with red cabbage or one of the famous flaky strudels. Then take a look at **Cooking with Nuts** and make a cream-clad chestnut Mont Blanc or a batch of crunchy walnut bread.

If you have a party in mind, the **Menus** in this Volume include two special dinner menus and a simpler one centered on turkey. Buffet dinner for a dozen need be no problem with the help of our menu and timetable, and the feature on **Ideas for Brunch** will inspire you to invite any number of guests. Have a ball in the kitchen and Bon Appétit!

Anne Willan

Stuffed pheasant en cocotte is served with braised celery and château potatoes (recipe is on page 12)

PHEASANT OR STEAK MAKES A LUXURY MENU

Pheasant is the suggested entrée for a very special dinner, or serve a simple Club steak. Whichever you choose, add one of the appetizers and dessert and you will have an ensemble to please the most exacting palate.

This elegant bird demands an elegant wine. An excellent red from northern Burgundy fits that description and few are better than those from the village of Chambolle Musigny. Its wines display the warmth and charm of any fine Burgundy, but they also possess a refinement and delicacy less often found. From California, buy the best obtainable Pinot Noir and try to get a bottle at least five years old.

Eggs Chimay
or
Scallop Chowder

Stuffed Pheasant en Cocotte
or
Club Steak au Naturel

Château or Baked Potatoes
Braised Celery Green Beans

Tarte aux Pommes à l'Orange
(Apple & Orange Flan)

Red Wine – Chambolle Musigny (Côte de Nuits)
or Pinot Noir (California)

TIMETABLE

Morning
Prepare and bake flan shell; fill and glaze. Cover and keep flan at room temperature.
Prepare all vegetables and keep in cold water.
Bone pheasant and make stuffing; cover both and keep in refrigerator.
Hard cook eggs, make stuffing and fill them. Cover and keep at room temperature.

Assemble equipment and ingredients for final cooking from 6:15 for dinner around 8 p.m.

Order of Work

6:30
Fill and truss the pheasant; begin to cook.
Braise the celery.

7:15
Cook potatoes *and green beans*, and keep warm.
Coat the eggs with the breadcrumbs, deep fry them and drain.

7:45
Transfer the pheasant to a platter and keep warm; prepare gravy and spoon over bird.
Set oven at hot (400°F).
Reheat chowder and add scallops.

7:55
Reheat eggs in oven.

8:00
Serve appetizer.
Steaks are best cooked just before serving.

You will find that **cooking times** given in the individual recipes for these dishes have sometimes been adapted in the timetable to help you when cooking and serving this menu as a party meal.

Appetizer

Eggs Chimay

8 hard-cooked eggs
$\frac{1}{4}$ cup seasoned flour (made with $\frac{1}{4}$ teaspoon salt and pinch of pepper)
1 egg, beaten to mix
$\frac{1}{2}$ cup dry white breadcrumbs
deep fat (for frying)
fried parsley (for garnish) – optional
2 cups tomato sauce (to serve)

For filling
3 tablespoons butter
1 onion, finely chopped
2 cups ($\frac{1}{2}$ lb) mushrooms, finely chopped
3 tablespoons flour
$\frac{1}{2}$ cup stock or milk
1 tablespoon chopped mixed herbs (parsley, thyme, chives)
salt and pepper
1 egg yolk

Fat thermometer (optional)

Method
To make the filling: in a skillet melt the butter and cook the onion until soft. Add mushrooms and cook over fairly high heat until most of the moisture has evaporated. Take from heat, stir in the flour, pour on the stock or milk and bring to a boil, stirring. Take the pan from the heat and add the herbs and seasoning.

Peel the eggs and cut them in half lengthwise. Scoop out the yolks, work them through a sieve and add to the mushroom mixture. Stir in the raw egg yolk – the mixture should be stiff but not too dry.

Wash and dry the halved egg whites and fill with mushroom mixture, joining the halves to form a whole egg. Roll in seasoned flour, then in beaten egg and breadcrumbs.

Fry the eggs in hot deep fat (350°F on a fat thermometer) until golden brown. Drain well on paper towels and garnish with fried parsley, if you like. Heat the tomato sauce and serve it separately.

If more convenient, these eggs may be deep fried 1–2 hours before serving, then reheated in a hot oven (400°F) for about 5 minutes.

Fill the halved egg whites with the mushroom mixture and reshape them

Fried Parsley
Thoroughly wash and dry a small bunch of parsley and tie with a long string. After frying food, let the fat cool a little before lowering in the parsley. Stand back as it will spit. After 30 seconds, or when spluttering stops, lift out parsley with the string. Discard stems and drain the sprigs on paper towels.

A luxury menu

Eggs Chimay are garnished with fried parsley before serving

Alternative appetizer

Scallop Chowder

$\frac{3}{4}$ lb sea scallops
$\frac{1}{4}$ cup rice
2 tablespoons butter
1 medium onion, finely chopped
4–5 slices of bacon, diced
4–5 stalks of celery, finely sliced
1 can (8 oz) tomatoes
about 1 quart boiling water
large pinch of saffron (infused in 2 tablespoons hot water for 30 minutes)
salt
black pepper, freshly ground
1 tablespoon chopped parsley

To strengthen the flavor of the chowder, $\frac{1}{4}$ cup white wine may be added in place of the same amount of boiling water.

Method

Soak the rice in cold water to cover for about 30 minutes, then drain.

In a large saucepan melt the butter, add the onion and bacon and fry gently for a few minutes. Add the rice and fry 2–3 minutes longer or until the rice looks transparent. Add the celery, tomatoes, boiling water (or boiling water and wine) and saffron. Season with salt and pepper, partially cover the pan and simmer 15–20 minutes or until the rice is very tender.

Slice the scallops and add to the soup. Taste for seasoning and simmer 2–3 minutes longer. If the chowder is too thick, add more liquid. Just before serving, stir in the chopped parsley.

Entrée

Stuffed Pheasant en Cocotte

4–5 lb pheasant
black pepper, freshly ground
$\frac{1}{4}$ teaspoon ground allspice (optional)
$\frac{1}{4}$ cup butter
6 tablespoons sherry
1 can (8 oz) Italian-type plum tomatoes

For stuffing
1 small onion, finely chopped
2 tablespoons butter
$\frac{1}{4}$ lb ground veal
$\frac{3}{4}$ cup fresh white breadcrumbs
$\frac{1}{2}$ cup ($\frac{1}{4}$ lb) chicken livers
$\frac{1}{4}$ teaspoon thyme or marjoram
salt and pepper

Trussing needle and string

Method

Slit the skin of the pheasant down the back and bone the carcass but leave in the wing bones and drumsticks (see box, right). When boned, lay the bird flat on a board with the cut side up, season with pepper and sprinkle with allspice, if you like.

To prepare the stuffing: cook the onion in the butter until it is soft but not browned. Transfer to a bowl and add ground veal and breadcrumbs. Remove any ducts from the chicken livers before slicing them as thinly as possible and add to the stuffing mixture with herbs and seasoning; mix well.

Stuff the pheasant, sew up, reshape and truss the bird (see Volume 1).

Heat a heavy flameproof casserole, add the $\frac{1}{4}$ cup butter and put the bird in, breast side down. Brown the pheasant on all sides over a low heat. Add half the sherry, heat and flame it. Cook for several minutes until there is a sticky brown glaze on the bottom of the pot.

Crush tomatoes lightly with a fork and spoon them around the pheasant. Season, cover with a piece of foil and the lid. Cook over a low heat or in a moderate oven (350°F) for 45–60 minutes or until the meat shrinks from the bones and a meat thermometer inserted in the center of the bird registers 170°F.

Transfer the pheasant to a warm platter, discard the trussing string and keep warm.

Work the remaining contents of the casserole through a strainer and add the remaining sherry. Transfer this sauce to a small pan, bring to a boil and pour it around the pheasant. Serve with château potatoes and braised celery (recipe is on page 14).

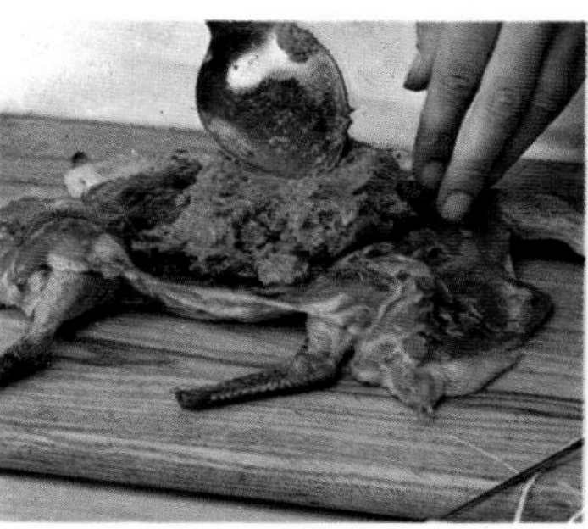

Stuff the partly boned pheasant with the herb, veal and chicken liver stuffing

Carefully sew the stuffed pheasant together, then reshape; truss it with string

To Bone a Pheasant

With a sharp knife, slit the skin along the backbone. Work the skin and flesh from here with a small knife until the leg joint is reached. Sever it.

Hold the end of the ball and socket joint firmly in one hand. Cut away flesh with a knife and scrape the thigh bone clean, always working from inside of the leg. Now cut thigh bone away from the flesh and drumstick and discard it. Repeat this cleaning process with the other leg.

Sever the wing joint from the carcass, leaving the bone attached to pheasant meat. Still using a knife, separate the white meat from the breastbone, leaving the carcass intact; stop there. Now free the other wing and breast.

Carefully cut away skin from the top of the breastbone without splitting the skin; this keeps both sides of the bird attached and in one piece for stuffing.

A luxury menu

Hot scallop chowder makes a good alternative appetizer on a chilly evening

Alternative entrée

Club Steak au Naturel

Club or New York strip steaks ($\frac{3}{4}$–1 inch thick each)
2–3 tablespoons butter
black pepper, freshly ground
$\frac{1}{4}$ cup sherry
bunch of watercress (optional)

Method

If necessary, trim the steaks of excess fat. Heat a large heavy skillet, put in about $\frac{1}{2}$ tablespoon butter and when it melts and foams put in the steaks. Fry over high heat for about 2 minutes on each side (for rare steak), turning the steaks only once. Season with a generous amount of pepper after turning. Transfer to a warm platter.

Lower the heat, cool the skillet slightly and deglaze the pan (dissolve juices) with the sherry. Pour this liquid over the steaks, add the rest of the butter to the skillet, cook until it is nut-brown (noisette) and pour at once over the meat.

Serve immediately with baked or château potatoes and green beans. Garnish the platter with watercress, if you like.

Club steak, pan fried and sauced with sherry is a simple alternative entrée

Accompaniment to entrées

Braised Celery

bunch of celery
1 large onion, diced
1 large carrot, diced
2 tablespoons butter
1 cup well-flavored stock
salt and pepper
bouquet garni

Method

Wash celery and slice off some of the leaves. Split the bunch in four and blanch in boiling salted water; drain.

In a large flameproof casserole sweat the onion and carrot in butter by covering tightly with foil and the lid and cooking over low heat until vegetables are soft but not brown.

Put the celery, stock, salt, pepper and the bouquet garni in with the vegetables. Cover and braise for 1–1$\frac{1}{2}$ hours or until tender in a moderately low oven (325°F), basting from time to time. When cooked, the sauce should be well reduced and the celery glazed.

Strain the sauce and pour over the celery in a vegetable dish.

Dessert

Tarte aux Pommes à l'Orange (Apple and Orange Flan)

For French flan pastry
scant 1 cup flour
$\frac{1}{4}$ cup sugar
2 egg yolks
$\frac{1}{4}$ cup butter
$\frac{1}{2}$ teaspoon vanilla

For filling
5–6 tart apples, pared, cored and sliced
3–4 tablespoons sugar
grated rind of 2 oranges

To finish
2 navel oranges
$\frac{1}{4}$ cup apricot jam glaze

8–9 inch flan ring

Method

To make French flan pastry; sift the flour onto a board or marble slab. Make a well in the center and put in the sugar, egg yolks, butter and vanilla. Work the mixture in the well to a paste with the fingertips. Then draw in the surrounding flour and work with the whole hand to form a smooth dough. Chill for at least 30 minutes.

Set oven at moderately hot (375°F).

Roll out the pastry dough and line flan ring.

To bake blind: fit a piece of wax paper or foil into the flan shell and pour in dry beans or rice to keep the sides firm. Bake flan shell in heated oven for 15–20 minutes or until the pastry is golden. Remove paper and bean or rice filling after 10–12 minutes baking

Apple and orange flan, made with French flan pastry, is a delicious dessert

so the pastry can brown all over.

To prepare the filling: put the apples into a well-buttered pan, cover with a tight-fitting lid and cook over low heat until the apples form a pulp. Work this through a sieve or food mill or purée in a blender and return the purée to the pan with sugar and orange rind. Cook, stirring constantly, until the mixture is thick. Transfer to a bowl and cool slightly.

Fill the baked flan shell with the apple purée, smoothing over the top with a spatula. With a serrated-edge knife, cut the rind and white pith from the oranges, slice them across the sections and arrange in overlapping circles on top of the apple purée. Melt the apricot jam glaze, brush over the oranges and leave the flan to cool and set.

Apricot Jam Glaze

In a saucepan put 12 oz apricot jam with the juice of $\frac{1}{2}$ lemon and 2 tablespoons water and bring slowly to a boil. Stir until melted, simmer 5 minutes, strain and return to the pan. Boil 5 minutes longer and pour into a jar for storage. If for immediate use, continue boiling until thick.

With your fingertips, work the ingredients to a paste before drawing in flour for pastry

Classic oyster stew is sprinkled with paprika before serving steaming hot

SHELLFISH (2)

From the lordly lobster to the humble clam, shellfish are universal favorites and their delicate flavors blend very well with rich ingredients like wine, cream and butter. Never overcook shellfish because it becomes tough, stringy and tasteless; it is best when cooked and served at once, so keep it waiting over low heat, or reheat gently only when absolutely necessary.

Thanks to freezing, shrimps, crab meat and lobster tails are available throughout the year but supplies of oysters and the much neglected mussel fluctuate in different areas and, of course, according to the season.

Live lobsters can always be found in specialty markets but supplies and prices vary according to the weather and the time of year.

Recipes for scallops, crabs and clams and more suggestions for shrimps were given in Volume 3.

LOBSTER

Lobster is a luxury and deserves careful cooking with the best ingredients.

Two kinds of lobster are available here – the greenish-blue clawed lobster that turns bright red when cooked, and the spiny or rock lobster with a brownish red shell and no claws.

The colder the water, the darker and rougher the shell of a spiny lobster and the better the flavor; the clawed lobster from cold northern climates is generally regarded as superior in flavor and texture.

Hen lobsters are valued for the red coral (roe) used to color and thicken sauces and soups. The hen lobsters are hard to distinguish from the cock lobsters, and it is illegal to sell them once the coral has extruded from their shells. However, a lobster has 2 small feelers under the body at the junction of the main shell and the tail; in a hen lobster these are soft and feathery, in a cock lobster they are firm.

Choose live lobsters that are heavy for their size and move strongly; lobsters stored in a tank have less flavor than those taken straight from the sea.

A 1–1½ lb lobster serves one person; large lobsters are also available and they are more meaty, but when over 3 lb, they can be tough.

The flavor of live lobsters is incomparable and the price high; even in fall or spring when the supply is greatest, live lobsters are very expensive. Frozen lobster tails, many of them imported, are also expensive, but good for adding to sauces or serving with other shellfish. They, too, must be cooked carefully or they can be stringy. Cooked lobster meat is also available fresh, frozen and canned.

To Kill a Live Lobster

Either plunge it into boiling water or court bouillon or pierce the head with a knife. Lobster should be killed and cooked by boiling if it is to be split and served plain either hot or cold.

However, many recipes call for the lobster meat to be sautéed or cooked in some other way. To avoid cooking lobster meat twice, the lobster must be killed by piercing through the back of the head, splitting and then extracting the raw meat. If lobster meat is cooked twice, it becomes tough and stringy.

To Kill a Lobster with a Knife

Lay the lobster flat on a board, hard shell up, with the head facing to the right, tail to the left; cover the tail with a cloth. Hold lobster firmly behind the head with your left hand, away from the claws, and with the point of a sharp chopping knife, pierce down to the board through the cross mark that lies on the center of the head.

To Boil a Lobster

Rinse it quickly in cold water. In a pan bring to a boil enough court bouillon or salted water to cover the lobster and put it in. Cover pan, bring back to a boil and simmer gently, allowing 12–15 minutes for a 1–1½ lb lobster, 18 minutes for a 2 lb one and 18 minutes and 3 minutes more per lb for larger lobsters.

When cooked, the lobster will be bright red.

To Split and Clean a Cooked or Uncooked Lobster

Cut through the top part of the head, turn the lobster around and continue to cut through the rear part of the body and down through the tail. Open the 2 halves on the board and discard the small membrane sac that lies in the top of the head and the dark thread (intestinal tract) that runs down the tail. Do not throw away the greenish liver (tomalley) in the body as this is a delicacy.

To serve a Lobster Hot

Take the pan from the heat, drain the lobster, split and clean it. Serve with melted butter and lemon wedges and give each person a small three-pronged fork and a nutcracker or mallet to crack the claws.

To Serve a Lobster Cold

Leave the lobster to cool in the liquid. Drain, split, clean and dress it and serve with mayonnaise and a garnish of lettuce leaves, tomatoes and hard-cooked egg.

To Dress a Cooked Lobster to Serve Cold

Split the lobster in half, remove the head sac and intestinal tract and twist off the claws. Crack them and carefully lift out the meat, removing the piece of membrane that lies down the middle of the claw. Twist the legs or snip them off with scissors.

With the handle of a wooden spoon, roll over the legs to push out the meat, then fit one into another to form a circle. This makes a good base to set the half shells on for serving.

Watchpoint: if time is short, omit the rolling out of the legs; they can be used for garnish only.

With the point of a small knife, loosen and lift out the tail meat, cut it diagonally into thick slices or 'scallops' and replace, rounded side up, in the opposite half of the shell. Arrange the claw and leg meat in the body shells and set the lobster on the leg circle in the serving dish. Garnish with watercress and serve mayonnaise separately.

Court Bouillon for Shellfish

For 2 quart quantity: in a kettle large enough to hold the shellfish, melt 2 tablespoons butter and cook 4 sliced onions and 2 sliced carrots until soft. Add the juice of 1 lemon, a large bouquet garni, 12 peppercorns, 2 quarts water, 1½ cups white wine, ½ teaspoon salt. Simmer 15–20 minutes. Strain before use.

To split an uncooked lobster, cut through the top part of the head, then turn the lobster around and cut through the body and tail

Lobster Thermidor

4 live lobsters (1–1¼ lb each)
¼ cup oil
6 tablespoons butter
4 shallots, finely chopped
1 cup white wine
2 teaspoons chopped fresh or 1 teaspoon dried tarragon
2 teaspoons chopped fresh or 1 teaspoon dried chervil
béchamel sauce, made with ¼ cup butter, ¼ cup flour, 2 cups milk (infused with slice of onion, 6 peppercorns, blade of mace and bay leaf)
¼ cup heavy cream
1 teaspoon Dijon-style mustard
¼ cup grated Parmesan cheese
salt and pepper

To finish
¼ cup browned breadcrumbs
¼ cup melted butter
bunch of watercress (for garnish)

If possible use fresh herbs as they give a better flavor. This dish can be prepared in the morning and left ready to be reheated and browned. It will then take 12–15 minutes to brown in a hot oven (400°F).

Method

Kill the lobsters with a knife, split them in half, discard the head sacs and intestinal tracts and crack the claws.

In a large skillet or roasting pan, heat the oil and ¼ cup of the butter and put in the lobsters, cut side down. Cover pan with a lid or foil and cook gently for 12–15 minutes or until the lobsters are red. Turn them once.

In a small saucepan, cook the shallot in remaining butter for ½ minute, add the wine and herbs and boil until reduced by half. Stir this mixture into the béchamel sauce and keep warm.

Take out the lobsters and strain any juice into the sauce. Stir well, add the cream, simmer 2–3 minutes, then take from the heat and mix in the mustard and half the cheese. Season, cover and set aside.

Remove the lobster meat from the claws, legs and body, chop it, mix with ¼ cup sauce and put into the body shells. Cut the tail meat into 'scallops', put 1 tablespoon sauce in the tail shells and replace the 'scallops', rounded side up. Place the shells on a baking sheet, wedging them with a piece of potato or a circle of leg shells.

Coat the lobsters with the remaining sauce, combine the crumbs and remaining cheese and scatter on top. Sprinkle with melted butter and bake in a hot oven (400°F) for 7–10 minutes or until brown. Garnish with watercress and serve very hot on a folded white napkin.

Lobster thermidor, coated with sauce, is sprinkled with cheese before browning

Lobster Newburg

2 live lobsters ($1\frac{1}{4}$–$1\frac{1}{2}$ lb each) or 1 live lobster ($2\frac{1}{2}$–3 lb) or 3 cups ($1\frac{1}{2}$ lb) cooked lobster meat
2 quart quantity of court bouillon
3–4 tablespoons butter
salt and pepper
$\frac{1}{2}$ cup brandy or Madeira
boiled rice (for serving)

For sauce
2 cups heavy cream
6 egg yolks, beaten to mix
5–6 tablespoons butter
$\frac{1}{2}$ teaspoon paprika (optional)

Lobster Newburg is an exception to the rule that hot lobster dishes should always be made with a live lobster as it is also good with ready-prepared lobster meat. If using cooked meat, gently warm it in the rich creamy sauce. If you use fresh lobster for this dish, try to pick a hen lobster as the coral gives an attractive pink color to the sauce.

Method
In a kettle boil live lobsters in court bouillon, allowing 15–18 minutes for the small ones or 21–24 minutes for a large one. Cool in the liquid.

Take the lobsters out of the pan, cut down each side of the soft shell under the tail with scissors and peel off the hard shell, keeping the tail meat in one piece. Cut it into 'scallops', discarding the head sac and intestinal tract. Crack the claws and legs, split the body shell and remove all meat.

Thickly butter a skillet or sauté pan, put in the lobster meat, season, cover and heat gently for 2–3 minutes. Add the brandy or Madeira and flame. Take from heat.

To make the sauce: in a bowl stir the cream into the egg yolks. If using paprika, first fry it in 1 tablespoon of the butter, then add to the cream and egg yolks with the coral, if any, and remaining butter in small pieces. Season well, pour over the lobster and heat slowly, shaking and swirling the pan gently until the sauce is thick and creamy.

Watchpoint: do not let it boil or it will curdle.

If you prefer, heat the sauce in the top of a double boiler until it thickens slightly before adding it to the lobster meat.

The lobster in the sauce may be kept hot in a double boiler or water bath for no more than 20 minutes. Serve with boiled rice.

Lobster Coral
If a split lobster has coral (this looks black when the lobster is uncooked and red when cooked), remove it, mash with 1 tablespoon butter on a plate with a fork and work it through a strainer. Stir into a lobster sauce just before removing it from the heat.

To flame, heat the brandy, rum, sherry or other liquor called for in the recipe until very hot. Set a match to it and cook until the flame dies. This burns off the harsh-flavored alcohol and helps the food over which the liquor has been poured to absorb the mellow flavor.

Wine can also be flamed but this is usually done in a separate pan and then added to the food.

Boiled Rice

Allow $\frac{1}{4}$ cup rice per person and boil at least 3 quarts water for every cup of rice. Add salt and slice of lemon to give flavor and whiteness. Sprinkle in the rice, stir with a fork to prevent it from sticking and boil steadily for 12–15 minutes or until the rice is just tender.

To stop the rice cooking, tip it at once into a colander and drain. Rinse thoroughly with hot running water to wash away any remaining starch, making several draining holes in the rice with the handle of a wooden spoon.

Transfer the rice to a large tray or platter, spread it out and let stand in a warm place or in a very low oven to dry for at least 15 minutes before serving, turning occasionally with a fork.

Lobster Gratiné

4 live lobsters (1–$1\frac{1}{4}$ lb each)
$\frac{1}{4}$ cup oil
$\frac{1}{4}$ cup butter
4 shallots, finely chopped
$1\frac{1}{2}$ cups white wine
béchamel sauce, made with 3 tablespoons butter, 3 tablespoons flour, 2 cups milk (infused with slice of onion, 6 peppercorns, blade of mace and bay leaf)
$\frac{1}{2}$ cup heavy cream
salt and pepper

To finish
$\frac{1}{4}$ cup browned breadcrumbs
$\frac{1}{4}$ cup grated Parmesan cheese
$\frac{1}{4}$ cup melted butter

This dish can be prepared in the morning to reheat and brown later. It will then take 12–15 minutes to brown in a hot oven (400°F).

Method
Kill the lobsters with a knife, split them in half, discard head sac and intestinal tract and crack the claws.

In a large skillet or roasting pan heat the oil and butter and put in lobsters, cut side down. Cover with a lid or foil and cook gently 3–4 minutes. Then bake in a moderate oven (350°F) for 10–15 minutes or until the lobsters are bright red; cool slightly.

Add the shallots to the wine and boil until it is reduced by half, stir into the béchamel sauce and strain in the juice from the lobster pan. Bring to a boil, add cream and season. Simmer sauce until it coats the back of a spoon. Take the lobster meat from the shell, chop the claw and leg meat and mix with $\frac{1}{2}$ cup sauce.

Slice the tail meat into 'scallops', pour a little of the sauce into the halved shells, place the claw and leg meat in the body shell and arrange the 'scallops' in the tail. Coat the lobsters with remaining sauce.

Mix the breadcrumbs and cheese, scatter over the lobsters and sprinkle with melted butter. Bake in a hot oven (400°F) for 7–10 minutes or until brown. Serve very hot.

Lobster Parisienne

4 live lobsters (1 ¼–1 ½ lb each)
2 quart quantity court bouillon (see box, page 18)
½ cup diced cooked carrots
½ cup diced cooked turnips
½ cup cooked peas
½ cup diced cooked green beans
bunch of watercress (for garnish)

For green mayonnaise
1 ½ cups mayonnaise
1 cup fresh herbs (parsley, tarragon, dill, watercress)

Method

In a kettle boil the lobsters in court bouillon for 15 minutes and cool in the liquid.

To make green mayonnaise: cook the herbs in boiling water for 2–3 minutes and drain them. Work through a sieve and stir into the mayonnaise or purée the herbs with the mayonnaise in a blender. Mix about half the green mayonnaise with the vegetables.

Drain the lobsters, split them in half and remove the meat from the shells, discarding the head sac and intestinal tract.

Fill the shells with the vegetable salad, arrange the lobster meat on top and coat with remaining mayonnaise. Garnish with watercress.

Deviled Lobster

4 live lobsters (1–1 ¼ lb each)
6 tablespoons butter
½ cup sherry
salt and pepper
bunch of watercress (for garnish)
boiled rice (for serving)

For devil sauce
2 tablespoons Worcestershire sauce
2 teaspoons tomato paste
2 teaspoons tarragon vinegar
1 tablespoon finely chopped onion
1–2 cloves of garlic, crushed
4 slices of lemon, cut in half
black pepper, freshly ground
2 bay leaves
1 cup red wine
1 cup court bouillon (see box, page 18), or ½ cup clam juice and ½ cup water (mixed)
3 tomatoes, peeled, seeded and cut in strips
½ cup heavy cream

Method

To make the devil sauce: in a kettle put all ingredients for the sauce, except the tomatoes and cream, cover and simmer 10–15 minutes. Discard the lemon slices and bay leaves and reserve the sauce.

Kill the lobsters with a knife, split them in half, discard the head sac and intestinal tract and crack the claws.

In a large skillet or roasting pan melt the butter and sauté the lobsters, cut side down, for 5 minutes. Add the sherry, bring to a boil and flame it. When the flame dies, add a cup of devil sauce, cover with the lid or foil and cook gently on top of the stove or in a moderate oven (350°F) for 10–15 minutes or until the lobsters are red.

Take out the lobsters, remove the meat from the claws, legs and tail, slice it and replace in the shell. Arrange on a hot platter.

Add the remaining devil sauce to the pan, bring to a boil, add the tomatoes and cream and adjust seasoning. Spoon over the lobsters, garnish with watercress and serve boiled rice separately.

Lobster Andalouse

4 live lobsters (1–1 ¼ lb each)
2 quart quantity court bouillon (see box, page 18) or salted water
1 ½ teaspoons paprika
¼ cup vinaigrette dressing
salt and pepper
3 tablespoons tomato juice or 1 slice of canned pimiento with 2 tablespoons tomato juice
2–3 dashes of Tabasco
squeeze of lemon juice

To serve
bunch of watercress or 2 hearts of Boston lettuce, halved (for garnish)
boiled rice
1 ½ cups mayonnaise

Method

In a kettle boil the lobsters in court bouillon or salted water for 12–15 minutes and cool in the liquid. Drain and dress them, arrange on a platter and garnish with watercress or lettuce hearts.

Add the paprika to the vinaigrette dressing, season well and stir into rice with a fork.

Stir the tomato juice, Tabasco and lemon juice into the mayonnaise. If using pimiento, purée it with mayonnaise and tomato juice in a blender or work the pimiento through a sieve and add to the mayonnaise with the tomato juice.

Garnish the lobsters with watercress or lettuce and serve the mayonnaise mixture and rice separately.

Mayonnaise

2 egg yolks
¼ teaspoon salt
pinch of pepper
pinch of dry mustard
¾ cup oil
2 tablespoons wine vinegar

Makes 1 cup.

Method

In a bowl, beat the egg yolks and seasonings with a small whisk or wooden spoon until thick. Add the oil, drop by drop; when 2 tablespoons have been added, the mixture will be very thick. Stir in 1 teaspoon vinegar.

The remaining oil can be added more quickly (1 tablespoon at a time, beaten thoroughly between each addition until smooth, or in a thin steady stream if using an electric blender). When all the oil has been used, add the remaining vinegar with more seasoning to taste.

To thin and lighten mayonnaise, add a little hot water. For a coating consistency, thin with a little cream or milk.

Watchpoint: mayonnaise curdles easily so be sure to add the oil drop by drop at first, and continue adding it *very* slowly until very thick, after which you can speed up. If mayonnaise does curdle, start with a fresh yolk in another bowl and work well the seasonings. Then add the curdled mixture drop by drop. To lessen the chances of curdling, have all the ingredients at room temperature before starting.

To serve oysters Rockefeller, set them on the half shell on a bed of rock salt

OYSTERS

The most important feature of an oyster is its freshness and the size is no indication of the quality because there are so many different varieties – ranging from the delicate Long Island blue points to the Chesapeake Bay oysters and the tiny Olympias from Puget Sound.

Most gourmets agree with Diamond Jim Brady, who regularly consumed 5 dozen fresh oysters as an appetizer – it is hard to beat chilled oysters on the half shell served with lemon wedges and a sprinkling of freshly ground black pepper.

However, cooked oysters are an excellent alternative, whether fried, baked or simmered in a stew. They should be cooked very lightly, only until the edges curl; whenever possible, use the oyster liquor in a recipe because it is full of flavor.

The usual serving of oysters on the half shell is 6 per person; a pint of shucked oysters serves 4 people and they come in 2 sizes – standard and select.

Oysters Rockefeller originated in 1899 at Antoine's, the celebrated restaurant founded in New Orleans by M. Antoine Alciatore. According to legend, the recipe was named when one of the customers tasted it and said: 'Why this recipe is as rich as Rockefeller'.

Oysters Rockefeller

2 dozen oysters on the half shell
6 tablespoons butter
6 tablespoons finely chopped raw spinach
3 tablespoons finely chopped parsley
3 tablespoons finely chopped celery
3 tablespoons finely chopped scallion
5 tablespoons fine dry white breadcrumbs
a few drops of Tabasco
$\frac{1}{2}$ teaspoon salt
2 tablespoons Pernod or anisette

Rock salt

Be sure the oysters are thoroughly scrubbed before opening them.

Method

Melt the butter in a saucepan and stir in all the ingredients except the oysters. Cook over a low heat, stirring constantly, for 15 minutes. Purée in a blender or work through a food mill and set aside.

Put a layer of rock salt in 4 heatproof dishes or in 1 large heatproof dish and set the oysters on their half shells on top. Put a spoonful of the spinach mixture on each oyster. Broil 3–5 minutes or until the oysters are very hot. Serve at once.

Oyster and Mushroom Soup

$\frac{1}{2}$ pint shucked oysters, with their liquor
1 cup ($\frac{1}{4}$ lb) finely sliced mushrooms
$\frac{1}{4}$ cup butter
3 cups milk
$\frac{1}{2}$ cup heavy cream
salt and pepper
1 tablespoon chopped parsley (for garnish)

Method

Drain the oysters, reserving the liquor.

In a large saucepan melt the butter and sauté the oysters and mushrooms briskly until the edges of the oysters curl.

Add the milk, cream and oyster liquor with seasoning to taste. Bring just to a boil and spoon into bowls. Sprinkle each bowl with a little chopped parsley and serve at once.

Oyster Stew

1 pint shucked oysters, with their liquor
3 tablespoons butter
1 medium onion, chopped (optional)
2 stalks of celery, chopped (optional)
2 cups light cream
2 cups milk
salt and pepper
2 tablespoons chopped parsley
1 teaspoon paprika (for sprinkling)

Method

In a large saucepan melt the butter and fry the onion and celery, if using, until soft. Add the oysters and their liquor and cook until the edges curl.

Add the cream and milk with seasoning to taste, bring just to a boil and add the chopped parsley.

Serve the stew at once in a tureen or individual bowls and sprinkle with paprika.

Oysters Casino

2 dozen oysters on the half shell
juice of 1 lemon
$\frac{1}{3}$ cup butter
1 green pepper, cored, seeded and finely chopped
2 cloves of garlic, crushed
6 slices of bacon, cut in four

Rock salt

Be sure the oysters are thoroughly scrubbed before opening them.

Method

Put a layer of rock salt in 4 heatproof dishes or 1 large heatproof dish and set the oysters on their half shells on top. Sprinkle each oyster with a little lemon juice.

In a pan melt the butter and cook the green pepper and garlic until soft. Sprinkle this mixture on the oysters and lay a piece of bacon on top of each one. Bake in a very hot oven (450°F) for 5–7 minutes or until bacon is crisp. Serve at once.

Angels on horseback – oysters wrapped in bacon and broiled or baked – are an unusual appetizer or tempting cocktail hors d'oeuvre

Angels on Horseback

1 pint shucked select oysters
$\frac{1}{2}$–$\frac{3}{4}$ lb sliced bacon
4–6 slices of bread, crusts removed, cut in squares, toasted and buttered (optional)
bunch of watercress (for garnish)

Toothpicks

Serve angels on horseback as an appetizer or cocktail hors d'oeuvre.

Devils on horseback are prunes, pitted and wrapped in bacon, then broiled.

Method

Cut the bacon slices in half and drain the oysters. Wrap each oyster in a piece of bacon and secure it with a toothpick. Broil these rolls 2–3 minutes on each side or until bacon is crisp or bake in a hot oven (400°F) for 5–7 minutes.

To serve as an appetizer, remove the toothpicks, arrange the rolls on squares of toasted buttered bread and garnish the dish with watercress.

To serve as an hors d'oeuvre, serve on the toothpicks.

Broiled Oysters

2 dozen oysters on the half shell
$\frac{1}{4}$ cup melted butter
1 tablespoon Worcestershire sauce
salt and pepper
1 lemon, cut in wedges (for serving)

Rock salt

Be sure the oysters are thoroughly scrubbed before opening them.

Method

Put a layer of rock salt in 4 heatproof dishes or in 1 large heatproof dish and set the oysters on their half shells on top.

Sprinkle them with melted butter, Worcestershire sauce and a little seasoning. Broil 1–2 minutes or until the edges curl. Serve at once with lemon wedges.

Oyster Fritters

1 pint shucked oysters, with their liquor
$1\frac{1}{2}$ cups flour
2 teaspoons baking powder
salt and pepper
3 eggs, lightly beaten
$\frac{1}{2}$ cup milk
$\frac{1}{2}$ cup butter (for frying)

Method

Cut oysters into 2–3 pieces.

Sift the flour with the baking powder and seasoning into a bowl, make a well in the center and add the eggs and milk. Stir until mixed, then gradually draw in the flour to make a smooth batter. Add the oysters and their liquor.

In a skillet melt half the butter, add generous tablespoons of the oyster mixture and fry briskly until golden brown on both sides. Drain on paper towels and keep warm while frying the remaining batter in the rest of the butter. Serve with tartare sauce.

Tartare Sauce

2 hard-cooked eggs
1 uncooked egg yolk
salt and pepper
$1\frac{1}{2}$ cups oil
1–2 tablespoons wine vinegar
2 tablespoons chopped parsley
2 teaspoons chopped chives
2 teaspoons chopped capers or gherkin pickles

Method

Halve the hard-cooked eggs, scoop out the yolks and work them through a sieve. Add the uncooked egg yolk and seasoning. Beat well, then add the oil drop by drop, as for mayonnaise, stirring in 1 tablespoon vinegar when the sauce becomes very thick. If you like, do this in a blender.

When all the oil has been added, stir in the parsley, chives and capers or gherkin pickles and season to taste, adding more vinegar, if necessary.

If you like, stir in the shredded white of one of the hard-cooked eggs.

Creamed Oysters

1 pint shucked select oysters, with their liquor
2 tablespoons butter
3 tablespoons sherry
1 cup heavy cream
4 egg yolks, beaten to mix
1 tablespoon chopped chives
salt and pepper
4 slices of bread, crusts removed and toasted (for serving)

Method

Drain the oysters, reserving the liquor.

In a skillet melt the butter, add the oysters and sauté 1 minute or until the edges curl. Add the sherry and heat thoroughly.

Stir the cream into the egg yolks, add to the skillet with the oyster liquor and heat gently, stirring, until the mixture thickens.

Watchpoint: do not let it boil or it will curdle.

Add the chives, season to taste and spoon onto the toast. Serve at once.

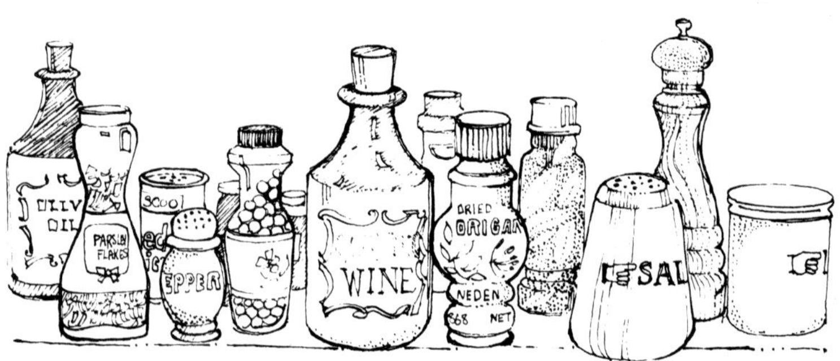

MUSSELS

Even though these small black shellfish grow along all our coasts, they are unfamiliar to most cooks. Mussels are available in good fish markets and are well worth looking for because they are inexpensive and full of flavor, whether eaten alone or combined in a sauce with other seafood.

Mussels are sold by the quart; 2–3 quarts serve 4 people. They must be scrubbed thoroughly before cooking and they are usually steamed open like clams. Discard any which do not open during steaming.

They can be served in the shell as for moules marinière – some cooks like to remove the top shell and the beard (gristle ring) around the mussel. Others serve them in their two shells.

Mussels are best eaten with a fork and fingers, with a spoon for the cooking liquid. Give each person a bowl for the empty shells. When the mussels are served with both shells, use an empty double shell as pincers to extract the meat easily. Or if picked up by the beard and popped into the mouth, pulling away the beard is easy.

Mussels can also be taken from the shell before serving to add to a soup or sauce.

Rinse the mussels, then scrub them well with a stiff brush. Discard any that don't close when tapped. Scrape off any weed clinging to shells; rinse

After soaking in fresh water, lift (do not tip) mussels into a colander so the sand is left behind in rinsing water

Strain liquid from the cooked mussels through cheesecloth to remove any remaining sand

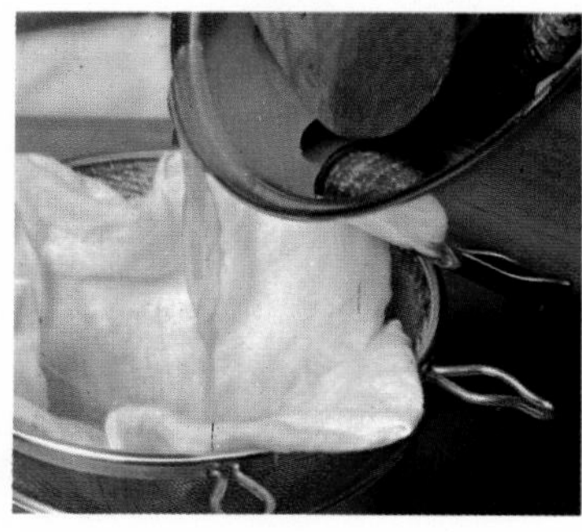

Mussels with Rice

3 quarts mussels
1 onion, sliced
1 carrot, sliced
bouquet garni
6 peppercorns
¾ cup white wine
¾ cup water
3 tomatoes, peeled, seeded and cut in strips
black pepper, freshly ground

For pilaf
1 cup rice
6 tablespoons butter
1 onion, chopped
2 stalks of celery, sliced
2–2½ cups water or chicken stock
pinch of saffron, soaked in ¼ cup boiling water for 30 minutes, or a little hot mussel liquor

Piece of cheesecloth

Method

Put the cleaned mussels in a kettle with the onion, carrot, bouquet garni and the peppercorns. Pour over the wine and water, cover and cook over medium heat, stirring once, for 5–7 minutes or until the shells open. Take pan from the heat and cool slightly.

Remove mussels from their shells, pull away the gristle ring and strain liquor through cheesecloth, reserving it. Mix mussels with the tomatoes and set aside.

To prepare the pilaf: melt 4 tablespoons of the butter in a flameproof casserole, add the onion and celery and cook 2–3 minutes until the onion is soft but not browned. Add the rice and stir over heat for 2–3 minutes more or until the grains are transparent.

Pour on 2 cups water or stock and add the saffron liquid or a little of the hot mussel liquor. Bring to a boil, cover pan and cook in a moderate oven (350°F) for 15 minutes. Add the remaining stock if the pan is dry and cook 5–7 minutes longer or until the rice is tender.

Carefully stir the mussels and tomatoes, with plenty of black pepper, into the rice with a fork. Dot the mixture with the remaining butter and, if the rice is dry, add 1 tablespoon more of the hot mussel liquor. Leave 10 minutes in a warm place before serving.

Moules Marinière

3 quarts mussels
1 onion, quartered
1 carrot, quartered
1 stalk of celery, sliced
large bouquet garni
¾ cup white wine (optional)
¾ cup water (or 1½ cups if no wine is used)
kneaded butter, made with 1 tablespoon butter and 2 teaspoons flour
2 tablespoons coarsely chopped parsley
pepper

Piece of cheesecloth

Method

Put the cleaned mussels in a kettle. Tuck the vegetables and bouquet garni down between the mussels. Pour over the liquid, cover pan tightly and cook over medium heat, stirring once, for 5–7 minutes or until the shells open. Take pan from heat and cool slightly. Lift out the mussels and keep warm.

Strain the cooking liquid through cheesecloth into a smaller pan. Whisk in the kneaded butter, a piece at a time, off the heat. Then bring to a boil, stirring until the mixture thickens, and cook gently for 4–5 minutes. Add the

→

parsley and season with pepper.

To serve, put the mussels into a soup tureen or individual bowls and pour over the thickened sauce.

Moules marinière – mussels are cooked in white wine or water and the liquid makes a sauce to spoon over them. They are best eaten with a fork and fingers; use a spoon for liquid and a bowl for empty shells

Snails with parsley butter are served in traditional escargot plates with the forks and tongs

SNAILS

Snails (escargots) do not fit neatly into any category, so they are included in shellfish, even though they live on land.

Snails are widely available in cans and are becoming increasingly popular, especially when prepared with garlic butter 'à la bourguignonne'. However, they blend equally well with less overwhelming flavors, particularly with wine and herbs.

In case you are tempted to gather your own snails, they need lengthy preparation before they are edible.

Periwinkles are snails that cling to rocks in intertidal areas. After soaking and boiling, extract the meat with a bent pin, then discard the tail.

Snails with Parsley Butter

24 canned snails
$\frac{1}{2}$ cup butter
1 clove of garlic, crushed
3 shallots, finely chopped
$\frac{1}{4}$ cup chopped parsley
$\frac{1}{2}$ teaspoon chervil
$\frac{1}{2}$ teaspoon thyme
1 tablespoon white wine
salt and pepper
French bread (to serve)

24 snail shells; 4 escargot plates or heatproof plates and rock salt

Method

Melt the butter, add the garlic and shallots and cook until soft. Take from heat, add the herbs, wine and seasoning and chill until set, stirring occasionally to distribute the flavorings evenly.

Fill the shells with the snails and seal each with a spoonful of the savory butter. Set the snails, opening up, on escargot plates or heatproof plates filled with a layer of rock salt and bake in low oven (300°F) for 20 minutes or until the butter begins to bubble. Serve very hot with French bread.

Note: to serve snails easily you should have the traditional escargot plates, forks and tongs.

ABALONE

Abalone is privately fished off the coast of California, but most commercial supplies come from Baja California.

The beautiful single shell is ear-shaped and the meat is sliced into fillets and pounded to tenderize it and bring out the delicate flavor, reminiscent of deep sea scallop.

Abalone is best coated with flour and sautéed quickly in butter for no more than 20 seconds each side. Never overcook it or it will become tough and inedible.

CONCH

Conch is a specialty of the Florida Keys. Like abalone, it has a striking multicolored single shell and the meat must be tenderized by pounding with a mallet. However, conch never becomes very tender and it is usually chopped for adding to chowder or ground for cakes or fritters.

SHRIMPS

It is hardly surprising that shrimps are the most popular shellfish. They are adaptable enough to blend readily with a wide variety of flavors and, because they freeze well, they are generally available.

All the following recipes are equally good with jumbo or medium shrimps.

Never simmer shrimps in the shell for more than 5 minutes; if shelled, 2–5 minutes simmering is sufficient depending on the size.

Shrimps Creole

$1\frac{1}{2}$ lb uncooked, peeled shrimps
3 tablespoons butter
1 tablespoon oil
2 onions, finely sliced
1 cup ($\frac{1}{4}$ lb) mushrooms, finely sliced
$\frac{1}{4}$ cup Marsala or sherry
1 green pepper, cored, seeded and chopped
2 teaspoons tomato paste
$1\frac{1}{2}$ cups heavy cream
$\frac{1}{2}$ teaspoon chili powder (or to taste)
salt and pepper
pilaf (for serving – see recipe for mussels with rice on page 26)

Method

Heat half the butter in a skillet with the oil and sauté the shrimps over high heat 2–3 minutes, depending on size, or until bright pink. Remove them, add the onion and cook until soft.

Add remaining butter and sauté the mushrooms until soft. Add the wine and pepper and cook gently for 2 minutes. Stir in the tomato paste, then the cream, chili powder and seasoning to taste. Bring this sauce just to a boil and add shrimps. Simmer gently for 2–3 minutes. Serve with pilaf.

Shrimps en Brochette

$1\frac{1}{2}$ lb uncooked, peeled shrimps
1 teaspoon chili powder
2 tablespoons wine vinegar
$\frac{1}{2}$ teaspoon thyme
1 teaspoon basil
2 shallots, finely chopped
salt and pepper
1 cup oil
$\frac{3}{4}$ cup dry white breadcrumbs
1 lemon, cut in wedges
pilaf (for serving – see recipe for mussels with rice on page 26)

4–8 kebab skewers

Method

Combine the chili powder, vinegar, herbs and shallot with seasoning to taste and beat in the oil. Spoon this mixture over the shrimps, cover and let marinate 12 hours in the refrigerator.

Drain the shrimps, coat thoroughly with breadcrumbs and spear them on the kebab skewers. Broil 2–4 minutes on each side depending on their size, basting with the marinade. Garnish with lemon wedges and serve with pilaf.

Serve shrimps Provençale in a tomato, mushroom and white wine sauce surrounded by rice

Shrimps Provençale

$1\frac{1}{2}$ lb uncooked, peeled shrimps
$\frac{1}{4}$ cup seasoned flour, made with $\frac{1}{4}$ teaspoon salt and pinch of pepper
3 tablespoons butter
boiled rice (for serving – see page 20)

For sauce
3 shallots, finely chopped
bouquet garni
$\frac{3}{4}$ cup white wine
3 tablespoons butter
2 tablespoons flour
1 clove of garlic, crushed
2 teaspoons tomato paste
$1\frac{1}{2}$ cups well-flavored chicken stock
salt and pepper
1 cup ($\frac{1}{4}$ lb) sliced mushrooms
3 tomatoes, peeled, seeded and coarsely chopped

Method

To prepare the sauce: in a small pan simmer the shallots with bouquet garni and wine until the liquid is reduced by half; reserve, discarding the bouquet garni.

Melt 2 tablespoons butter, stir in the flour and cook until straw-colored. Stir in the garlic, tomato paste, stock and seasoning, simmer 10–15 minutes and add the reduced wine. Cook 5 minutes longer, take from heat and stir in remaining butter in small pieces. Keep warm.

Toss the shrimps in the seasoned flour. Melt the butter in a skillet and sauté shrimps 3–4 minutes, depending on their size, until brown on all sides.

Arrange the boiled rice around a platter and pile the shrimps in the center; keep warm.

Add the mushrooms to the skillet, cook until tender, add them to the sauce with the tomatoes and taste for seasoning. Heat thoroughly without boiling and spoon over the shrimps.

Shrimps with Alabama Dip

1 lb uncooked, peeled large shrimps
fritter batter (made with $\frac{1}{4}$ cup flour, pinch of salt, 2 egg yolks, 1 tablespoon melted butter or oil, $\frac{1}{2}$ cup milk, 1 egg white)
deep fat (for frying)

For Alabama dip
$\frac{1}{2}$ green pepper, cored, seeded, chopped and blanched
4 stalks of celery, chopped
1 clove of garlic, crushed
$\frac{1}{2}$ cup mayonnaise (see page 21)
1 cup chili sauce
1 tablespoon grated horseradish
salt and pepper
dash of Tabasco

Wooden toothpicks

Method

Make the fritter batter and let stand 30 minutes. Mix together all the ingredients for the Alabama dip and set aside.

Dip the shrimps in batter and fry them, a few at a time, in hot deep fat (350°F on a fat thermometer) until golden brown. Drain them on paper towels and keep warm while frying the remaining shrimps.

Serve the shrimps hot, speared on toothpicks with the Alabama dip in a separate bowl.

Shrimps Sicilienne

1–$1\frac{1}{2}$ lb cooked, peeled shrimps
bunch of watercress (for garnish)

For rice molds
1 cup rice, boiled (see page 20)
$\frac{1}{3}$ cup slivered almonds
1 teaspoon paprika
$\frac{1}{4}$ cup vinaigrette dressing

For sauce
1 cup mayonnaise (see page 21)
2 slices of canned pimiento, drained
juice of 1 large orange
juice of 1 lemon
2 shallots, finely chopped
$\frac{1}{3}$ cup tomato purée

salt and pepper

4 custard cups

Method

Lightly oil the custard cups.

Soak almonds in warm water for 30 minutes (this makes them juicy like fresh nuts). Drain the almonds well on paper towels.

Add the paprika to the vinaigrette dressing and mix into the cooked rice with the almonds. Spoon the rice into the prepared custard cups and press down lightly.

To make the sauce: work the pimiento through a sieve and add to the mayonnaise with both the orange and lemon juice, shallot and tomato purée. Taste for seasoning.

Unmold the rice onto 4 individual plates and pile the shrimps around the bases of the molds. Spoon the sauce over the shrimps, garnish with watercress and serve.

CRAYFISH

These freshwater shellfish are found in the Midwest near the Great Lakes, particularly in Wisconsin, and around New Orleans, but unfortunately they are rarely available in markets. They look like very small lobsters and are a great delicacy because they taste like lobster and the meat is very tender.

They are best when thoroughly washed, then cooked for 5–7 minutes in court bouillon to cover.

Crayfish are served in the shell and a pair of scissors and a small three-pronged fork are a great help in extracting the meat.

To serve them hot, strain the court bouillon in which they were cooked and boil it to reduce by two-thirds. Add half this volume in butter, in small pieces, whisking it over gentle heat without boiling. Serve this sauce separately with the hot crayfish, allowing 1 dozen per person.

To serve crayfish cold, leave them in the court bouillon and serve them à la nage' (swimming) in the liquid, with mayonnaise separately, if you like.

Crayfish can also be substituted for shrimps, particularly in recipes with a delicate sauce.

HOT SOUFFLES, SOUFFLE OMELETS AND ROULADES

Hot soufflés are one of the tests of a good cook, but like many skills they present no problems if you follow the rules.

A soufflé is made with stiffly beaten egg whites that are folded into a flavored base mixture. When cooked, the soufflé mixture expands and puffs above the edge of the dish in which it is cooked. The basic mixture can be savory or sweet and flavored with almost any meat, chicken, fish, vegetables, fruit or sweet flavoring. It may be a purée or a creamy sauce and should be of a consistency that falls easily from a spoon.

Soufflés are delicate; the egg whites that make them rise must be folded very gently into the basic mixture to retain the maximum amount of air. Once mixed, a soufflé should be cooked as soon as possible and, when cooked, it must be served at once – if a soufflé overcooks 5 minutes or waits in a drafty room, it will be ruined.

The following soufflés are French-type mixtures; that is, they are cooked in a comparatively high oven so they are firm on the outside but still soft in the center. The soft center makes a type of sauce for the crisper outside, so that a separate sauce is rarely necessary. These soufflés take only 20–25 minutes to cook – you can wait for tardy guests before putting them into the oven.

Roulades and soufflé omelets are more robust variations on the soufflé theme, so you may like to try them before tackling the trickier classic soufflé.

Points to remember

1 Choose the right size soufflé dish – these come in so many sizes that they are best measured by volume (to check, simply fill the dish with a measured amount of water). The soufflé mixture should fill the dish about seven-eighths full before baking.

2 Prepare the dish by rubbing it generously with butter, then sprinkling it with browned breadcrumbs for a savory soufflé (or with sugar for a sweet soufflé), discarding the excess.

3 A perfect soufflé should rise above the dish without collapsing, but to be safe tie a collar of wax or silicone paper around the dish to hold the mixture as it rises. Cut a strip of doubled paper 6–7 inches wide and long enough to overlap about 3 inches around the dish. Make a 2 inch fold along the bottom. Butter the strip above this fold and wrap the band around the outside of the dish, with the folded piece at the base and turned in. This will keep the paper upright and firm. The buttered section of the paper should extend 3 inches above the level of the dish.

Tie the paper securely with string and set the dish on a baking sheet before filling it. Untie the string and peel off the paper just before serving.

4 The consistency of the basic mixture is important; it should be soft and drop easily from a spoon. If the mixture is too thin, the egg whites are very difficult to fold in; if it is too thick and sticky, the egg whites cannot raise it. Comparatively heavy mixtures like vegetable purées will never rise as much as light soufflés like cheese or vanilla.

5 The basic mixture must be highly seasoned to compensate for the bland egg whites added later.

6 Most basic mixtures can be prepared a few hours in advance, but the egg whites must be beaten at the last minute before folding into the basic mixture.

7 For most soufflé mixtures, one-third to one-half more egg whites are added than egg yolks. When the egg whites are beaten, their volume should at least equal the amount of basic mixture and will often exceed it. A soufflé should double in size during cooking.

8 Since the beaten egg whites make the soufflé rise, it is essential to beat them well. Ideally you should use a copper bowl and a balloon whisk since the shape of the bowl and the rounded whisk make it easy to beat in as much air as possible, and contact with the copper gives egg whites a close, smooth texture.

9 When adding the egg whites to most mixtures, heat the mixture to very warm but not hot. Add about one-quarter of the beaten egg whites and fold together very thoroughly. This lightens the basic mixture and the egg whites are cooked slightly so they remain firm. Then add remaining egg whites and fold together as lightly as possible.

The heavy basic mixture tends to fall to the bottom so, while folding, lift the mixture well from the bottom, turning the saucepan. Fold until the mixture is almost smooth but a few streaks of egg white remain.

Butter the top of the paper and rub inside the dish with butter; sprinkle with browned crumbs for savory soufflés or with sugar for sweet soufflés. Wrap around a band of paper with a 2 inch fold at the base and a 3 inch overlap at the top. Tie securely

Fold one-quarter of the egg whites into the basic soufflé mixture to lighten it; fold in remaining egg whites as lightly as possible

10 Preheat the oven to the required temperature and arrange the shelves so that the soufflé can be placed in the center of the oven with no shelf above it. This leaves plenty of room for it to rise. Do not cook anything else in the oven with the soufflé and avoid opening the oven door until the soufflé is almost done.

11 Serve it at once – guests, not the soufflé, should be kept waiting. When cooked, the top of the soufflé should be evenly brown and firm to the touch.

Some cooks like to trace a circle with a knife around the top of the unbaked mixture so that the soufflé forms a central 'top hat' as it bakes.

Serve a soufflé with a large spoon, break the crust and scoop into the center so that each person has some of the soft center and firmer outside.

12 If, in case of emergency, a soufflé must be kept waiting, open the oven door and leave on the oven heat. The outer side of the soufflé will slowly shrivel but the inner side will stay puffed. After 5 minutes, turn soufflé halfway around so the shriveled side faces the heat. This procedure can be repeated once or twice, but is only recommended for a dire emergency.

A soufflé dish is circular with straight sides so that the soufflé mixture can rise straight up. The deeper the dish, the higher the mixture rises as it puffs. The classic soufflé dish is made of white ovenproof porcelain with ribbed sides but dishes also come decorated with flowers or fruit and vegetable patterns, or with a shiny gold or silver colored finish.

To make browned breadcrumbs: bake several crusts of white bread in a low oven until golden brown. Grind or work the crusts a few at a time in the blender. Sift the crumbs through a wire strainer to make them uniformly fine and store in a dry airtight container.

To Beat Egg Whites in a Copper Bowl

Always clean the copper bowl immediately before use – combine 2 tablespoons salt with 1–2 tablespoons vinegar or lemon juice in the bowl and rub with a cloth until the copper surface shines. Wash with warm water and dry very thoroughly. Any traces of dampness or grease on the whisk or bowl or any trace of yolk in the egg whites prevents them from stiffening when beaten.

Start whisking slowly in the bottom of the bowl then, as the egg whites break up, beat in larger and larger circles, lifting the whisk out of bowl to incorporate as much air as possible. When the whites hold a stiff peak, 'tighten' them by beating around and around as fast as possible for ½–1 minute, keeping the whisk in contact with the bowl.

If you have no copper bowl, use a stainless steel bowl; beat the whites only to a froth with a rotary beater or electric mixer, then continue beating by hand with a balloon whisk.

SAVORY SOUFFLES

Cheese Soufflé

½ cup grated cheese
3 tablespoons butter
2 tablespoons flour
1 cup milk
salt
pinch of cayenne
1 teaspoon prepared mustard
4 egg yolks
5–6 egg whites
1 tablespoon browned breadcrumbs

Soufflé dish (5 cup capacity)

Ideally the cheese for a soufflé should be a mixture of grated Parmesan and Gruyère. Otherwise use a dry sharp Cheddar.

Method

Prepare the soufflé dish with a paper collar; set oven at hot (425°F).

In a medium to large saucepan melt the butter, stir in the flour off the heat and pour in the milk. Season well and bring to a boil, stirring. Simmer 2 minutes, take from the heat and beat in the mustard, all but 2 tablespoons of cheese and the egg yolks, one at a time. Adjust seasoning – the mixture should be very highly seasoned.

Beat the egg whites until they hold a stiff peak. If necessary, warm the basic cheese mixture over low heat until very warm – do not let it get too hot or the cheese will become stringy.

Using a metal spoon fold, one-quarter of the egg whites into the cheese mixture, then add remaining egg whites and fold together as lightly as possible. Transfer carefully to the prepared soufflé dish.

Mix the breadcrumbs with the remaining cheese and sprinkle the top with this mixture. Bake at once in heated oven for 15–20 minutes or until the soufflé is puffed and brown. Remove the paper collar and serve at once.

Note: cheese soufflé mixture can be baked plain or it can be layered with cooked fish, meat or vegetables – this is an excellent way of using up leftovers.

Rich Cheese Soufflé

$\frac{1}{4}$ cup grated Parmesan cheese
$\frac{1}{4}$ cup grated Gruyère cheese
2 teaspoons potato starch or arrowroot
2 teaspoons butter
$\frac{1}{2}$ cup heavy cream
3 egg yolks
pinch of dry mustard
salt and pepper
5 egg whites

Soufflé dish (1 quart capacity)

This soufflé is tricky to make but it is much lighter and more delicate than a regular cheese soufflé.

Method

Prepare the soufflé dish (the paper collar is optional) and set oven at hot (425°F).

In a heavy saucepan mix the potato starch or arrowroot, butter and cream and cook over low heat, stirring constantly.

Watchpoint: just after the butter melts, the mixture will thicken; take from heat at once and do not let it boil or it will curdle.

Stir in the egg yolks, one at a time, and Parmesan cheese, half the Gruyère cheese and the mustard with salt and pepper to taste. Cook again, stirring, over very low heat until the mixture just begins to thicken; do not overcook or the cheese will become stringy.

Beat the egg whites until they hold a stiff peak and, using a metal spoon, fold one-quarter of them into the cheese mixture (if necessary warm it slightly beforehand). Add the remaining egg whites and fold together as lightly as possible.

Transfer the mixture to the prepared soufflé dish, sprinkle with remaining Gruyère cheese and bake at once in heated oven for 15–18 minutes or until the soufflé is puffed and brown. It will be very soft in the center. Remove the paper collar if used and serve at once.

Corn and Cheese Soufflé

1$\frac{1}{2}$ cups cooked corn kernels
$\frac{1}{2}$ cup grated cheese (preferably Gruyère and Parmesan, mixed)
$\frac{1}{4}$ cup heavy cream
pinch of cayenne
salt and pepper
5 egg yolks
7 egg whites

For béchamel sauce
$\frac{1}{4}$ cup butter
$\frac{1}{4}$ cup flour
1$\frac{1}{2}$ cups milk (infused with slice of onion, $\frac{1}{2}$ bay leaf, 6 peppercorns, blade of mace, few slices of carrot)

For mornay sauce
2$\frac{1}{2}$ tablespoons butter
2 tablespoons flour
2 cups milk
$\frac{1}{2}$ cup grated cheese (Parmesan and Gruyère, mixed)

Soufflé dish (1$\frac{1}{2}$ quart capacity)

Method

Prepare the soufflé dish with a paper collar and set oven at hot (425°F).

Make the béchamel sauce, take from the heat and stir in the cream, corn kernels, $\frac{1}{4}$ cup of the cheese, cayenne, salt and pepper to taste and the egg yolks, one at a time.

Beat the egg whites until they hold a stiff peak and, using a metal spoon, fold one-quarter of them into the corn mixture (if necessary, warm it slightly beforehand). Add the remaining egg white and fold together as lightly as possible.

Transfer the mixture to the prepared soufflé dish, sprinkle the top with remaining $\frac{1}{4}$ cup grated cheese and bake at once in heated oven for 15–20 minutes or until the soufflé is puffed and brown.

Meanwhile prepare the mornay sauce: melt the butter in a pan, remove from heat and stir in the flour. Pour on half the milk, blend until smooth, add the remaining milk and season lightly; bring to a boil over low to moderate heat, stirring constantly. Simmer 2 minutes, remove from heat and gradually stir in the grated cheese. Reheat but do not boil and taste for seasoning.

When the soufflé is baked, remove the paper collar and serve it immediately with the mornay sauce served separately. The mornay sauce is a great addition because if by any chance the soufflé is a little overcooked and dry, the sauce helps to add creaminess.

Mushroom Soufflé

2 cups ($\frac{1}{2}$ lb) mushrooms, finely chopped
2 tablespoons butter
1 tablespoon chopped mixed herbs (parsley, mint, chives)
salt and pepper
4 egg yolks
5–6 egg whites
1 tablespoon browned breadcrumbs
1 tablespoon grated Parmesan or dry sharp Cheddar cheese

For béchamel sauce
3 tablespoons butter
2 tablespoons flour
1$\frac{1}{2}$ cups milk (infused with slice of onion, $\frac{1}{2}$ bay leaf, 6 peppercorns, blade of mace, few slices of carrot)

Soufflé dish (5 cup capacity)

Method

Prepare the soufflé dish with a paper collar and set oven at hot (425°F).

In a skillet melt the butter and cook the mushrooms over fairly high heat for 4–5 minutes until the moisture has evaporated. Take from heat and stir in the herbs and seasoning. Make béchamel sauce. Stir into mushrooms. Beat in yolks, one at a time.

Beat the egg whites until they hold a stiff peak and, using a metal spoon, fold one-quarter into the mushroom mixture (if necessary, warm it slightly beforehand). Add the remaining egg white and fold together as lightly as possible.

Transfer the mixture to the prepared soufflé dish, combine the breadcrumbs and cheese and sprinkle the top with this mixture. Bake at once in heated oven for 15–20 minutes or until the soufflé is puffed and brown. Remove paper collar and serve at once.

Hot soufflés, soufflé omelets and roulades

Corn and cheese soufflé is ideal to serve for supper or as a light entrée with salad

Spinach Soufflé

$\frac{3}{4}$ lb fresh or 1 package frozen spinach
1 tablespoon butter
salt and pepper
pinch of grated nutmeg or ground mace
4 egg yolks
5–6 egg whites
1 tablespoon browned breadcrumbs
1 tablespoon grated Parmesan or dry sharp Cheddar cheese

For white sauce
3 tablespoons butter
$2\frac{1}{2}$ tablespoons flour
1 cup milk

Soufflé dish ($1\frac{1}{2}$ quart capacity)

This is a basic recipe for vegetable soufflés and other puréed vegetables can be used instead of spinach – for example, cauliflower, carrots, leeks or celery. Allow $1\frac{1}{4}$–$1\frac{1}{2}$ cups purée for the above quantity of sauce and, for a bland vegetable like broccoli, add 2 tablespoons grated Parmesan or dry sharp Cheddar cheese to the basic mixture.

Method

Prepare the soufflé dish (the paper collar is optional) and set oven at hot (425°F).

Trim and wash fresh spinach and cook in boiling salted water for 5 minutes or until tender or cook frozen spinach according to package directions. Drain and refresh under cold running water.

Purée the spinach: if using a sieve, work spinach through the sieve and cook it over moderate heat, stirring until it is dry. Add the 1 tablespoon butter and seasoning. If using a blender, dry spinach over moderate heat, add the butter and seasoning and then purée it with a little of the sauce.

Make the white sauce. Add it to the spinach with the nutmeg or mace and season to taste. Beat in the egg yolks one at a time.

Beat the egg whites until they hold a stiff peak and, using a metal spoon, fold one-quarter into the spinach mixture (if necessary, warm it beforehand). Add the remaining egg white and fold together as lightly as possible.

Transfer the mixture to the prepared soufflé dish, combine the breadcrumbs and cheese and sprinkle the top with this mixture. Bake at once in heated oven for 15–20 minutes or until the soufflé is puffed and brown and firm to the touch. Remove the collar if used and serve at once.

Italian Soufflé

2 tablespoons butter
2 tablespoons flour
1 cup milk
salt
pinch of cayenne
6 tablespoons grated Parmesan or dry sharp Cheddar cheese
$\frac{1}{2}$ teaspoon prepared mustard
3 egg yolks
4–5 egg whites
1 tablespoon browned breadcrumbs

Italian soufflé is made with alternate layers of spaghetti in a tomato-flavored sauce

For filling
$\frac{1}{3}$ cup uncooked spaghetti, broken into pieces
1 tablespoon butter
$\frac{1}{4}$ cup tomato sauce or tomato purée

Soufflé dish ($1\frac{1}{2}$ quart capacity)

Chopped cooked ham or mushrooms can be added to the spaghetti or used in place of it, if you like.

Method

Prepare the soufflé dish (the paper collar is optional).

To make the filling: simmer the spaghetti in salted water for 8–10 minutes or until just tender ('al dente'). Drain it, rinse with hot water and drain again.

Melt 1 tablespoon butter in a pan, add the spaghetti and toss over heat for 1 minute. Add the tomato sauce or purée, season well and stir with a fork until the spaghetti is well coated with tomato. Keep warm. Set oven at hot (425°F).

Make the soufflé mixture as for cheese soufflé, using all the cheese.

When ready, put enough of the soufflé mixture into the prepared soufflé dish to cover the base. Add half the spaghetti and cover this with half the remaining soufflé mixture. Add the remaining spaghetti, top it with the rest of the soufflé mixture and sprinkle with browned breadcrumbs.

Bake at once in heated oven for 15–20 minutes or until the soufflé is puffed and brown. Remove the paper collar if used and serve at once.

Fish Soufflé

1 lb flounder fillets
3 egg yolks
salt and pepper
pinch of ground mace
1 tablespoon heavy cream
4 egg whites
1 tablespoon browned breadcrumbs

For béchamel sauce
1 tablespoon butter
1 tablespoon flour
$\frac{3}{4}$ cup milk (infused with slice of onion, $\frac{1}{2}$ bay leaf, 6 peppercorns, blade of mace, few slices of carrot)

Soufflé dish (1 quart capacity)

This soufflé has a closer texture than the usual French soufflé and is cooked in a lower oven for a longer time so that it is fairly firm in the center. Serve with a sauce, such as curry hollandaise or a crab or lobster sauce.

Method

Prepare the soufflé dish with a paper collar and set oven at moderately hot (375°F).

Cut the flounder fillets into shreds.

To make the béchamel sauce: melt the butter in a pan, remove from heat and stir in the flour. Pour on half the infused milk through a strainer and blend until smooth. Add the remaining milk, season lightly, return to moderate heat and bring to a boil. Simmer 2 minutes, stirring continuously. Cool.

Pound the fish with a mortar and pestle until smooth, adding the sauce a little at a time, or purée the fish and sauce in a blender. Beat in the egg yolks one at a time and, if the mixture is not very smooth, work it through a sieve. Season, add the mace and stir in the cream.

Beat egg whites until they hold a stiff peak and, using a metal spoon, fold one-quarter of them into the cold fish mixture. Add remaining egg whites and fold together as lightly as possible.

Transfer the mixture to the prepared soufflé dish, sprinkle the top with breadcrumbs and bake at once in heated oven for 20–25 minutes or until the soufflé is brown and firm to the touch. Remove the paper collar and serve at once.

Curry Hollandaise

Make 1 cup hollandaise sauce (see Volume 2) and then add 1–2 teaspoons curry powder.

Crab soufflé

$\frac{3}{4}$ lb crab meat
2 tablespoons butter
2 shallots or scallions, finely chopped
1 teaspoon curry powder
1 teaspoon paprika
2 tablespoons light cream
1–2 tablespoons sherry
dash of Tabasco
salt and pepper
3 egg yolks
4 egg whites
2 tablespoons browned breadcrumbs
2 tablespoons grated Parmesan cheese

For béchamel sauce (see fish soufflé for method)
2 tablespoons butter
2 tablespoons flour
$\frac{3}{4}$ cup milk (infused with slice of onion, $\frac{1}{2}$ bay leaf, 6 peppercorns, blade of mace, few slices of carrot)

Soufflé dish (1 quart capacity)

Method

Prepare the soufflé dish with a paper collar and set oven at hot (425°F).

In a saucepan, melt the butter and sauté the shallots until soft. Add curry powder and paprika and cook 30 seconds. Take from the heat and stir in the crab meat with the cream and sherry. Make the béchamel sauce and beat it into the crab meat mixture with the seasonings and egg yolks. The mixture may be prepared 3–4 hours ahead of time up to this point.

Beat the egg whites until they hold a stiff peak and, using a metal spoon, fold one-quarter into the cold crab mixture to lighten it. Add remaining egg whites and fold together as lightly as possible.

Transfer the mixture to the prepared soufflé dish, combine the breadcrumbs with Parmesan cheese and sprinkle the top with this mixture. Bake at once in heated oven for 15–20 minutes or until the soufflé is puffed and brown. Remove the paper collar and serve at once.

Crab or Lobster Sauce

$\frac{1}{2}$ cup ($\frac{1}{4}$ lb) cooked crab or lobster meat
2 tablespoons butter
$1\frac{1}{2}$ tablespoons flour
1 teaspoon paprika
$\frac{3}{4}$ cup fish stock or $\frac{3}{8}$ cup bottled clam juice mixed with $\frac{3}{8}$ cup water
$\frac{3}{4}$ cup milk
1 tablespoon sherry
1 tablespoon heavy cream
salt and pepper

Method

Break up the crab or lobster meat with a fork and remove any membrane.

In a saucepan melt the butter, stir in the flour and cook over low heat for 30 seconds. Stir in the paprika and cook 30 seconds longer (take care not to scorch it).

Take pan from heat, stir in the fish stock or clam juice and water, return to heat and bring the sauce to a boil, stirring. Add the milk, bring back to a boil and simmer 2–3 minutes.

In a small pan heat the crab or lobster meat in the sherry and add to the sauce with the cream. Season to taste and serve.

Chocolate soufflé is sprinkled with confectioners' sugar to serve

SWEET SOUFFLES

A sweet soufflé is often made with a smooth light sauce base, not with a butter and flour roux like a savory soufflé. This smooth base gives a very creamy texture, particularly if arrowroot as well as flour is used for thickening.

To prepare a soufflé dish for a sweet mixture, before filling, remember to rub the dish generously with butter, then sprinkle with sugar, discarding the excess.

For other information, refer back to points to remember on page 34.

Chocolate Soufflé

4 squares (4 oz) semisweet chocolate, cut in small pieces
1½ cups milk
3 tablespoons sugar
½ teaspoon vanilla
1 tablespoon flour
2 teaspoons arrowroot
1 tablespoon butter
3 egg yolks
4 egg whites
1 tablespoon confectioners' sugar (for sprinkling)

Soufflé dish (1 quart capacity)

Method

Prepare the soufflé dish with a paper collar and set oven at hot (425°F).

Put the chocolate pieces in the top of a double boiler and melt over gentle heat, stirring. Add the milk, reserving ¼ cup, transfer to a saucepan and bring the milk and chocolate to a boil. Add the sugar and vanilla, cover and set aside.

Stir the reserved milk into the flour and arrowroot and mix to a smooth paste. Pour this into the chocolate milk mixture, return to heat and bring to a boil, stirring constantly. Boil 10 seconds, take from the heat, dot surface with the butter, cover and leave 5 minutes. Then stir to mix in the butter and beat in the egg yolks, one at a time.

Beat the egg whites until they hold a stiff peak and, using a metal spoon, fold one-quarter into the warm chocolate mixture. Add remaining egg white and fold together as lightly as possible.

Transfer the mixture to the soufflé dish and bake at once in heated oven for 15–20 minutes or until the soufflé is puffed. Remove the paper collar, sprinkle the top with confectioners' sugar and serve at once.

Vanilla Soufflé

1 vanilla bean or 1 teaspoon vanilla extract, or to taste
1¼ cups milk
3 tablespoons sugar
1 tablespoon flour
2 teaspoons arrowroot
2 tablespoons butter
3 egg yolks
4 egg whites
2 tablespoons confectioners' sugar (for sprinkling)

Soufflé dish (1 quart capacity)

Method

Prepare the soufflé dish with a paper collar and set oven at hot (425°F).

Scald 1 cup of the milk; if using vanilla bean, put it into the milk, cover and leave to infuse 15 minutes. Reheat milk to a boil, remove from the heat, remove vanilla bean and add sugar. If using vanilla extract, add to scalded milk.

Blend the remaining milk with the flour and arrowroot to make a smooth paste. Stir into the hot milk and bring to a boil, stirring constantly. Boil 2–3 seconds and remove from heat. Dot surface with butter, cover and let stand for 5 minutes.

Stir to mix in the butter and add more vanilla extract to taste. Beat in the egg yolks, one at a time. Beat the egg whites until they hold a stiff peak and, using a metal spoon, fold one-quarter of them into the yolk mixture. Add the remaining egg white and fold together as lightly as possible.

Transfer the mixture to the prepared soufflé dish and bake at once in heated oven for 18–20 minutes or until the soufflé is puffed and brown. Remove the paper collar, sprinkle the top with confectioners' sugar and serve at once.

Orange Soufflé

2 oranges
18 cubes of sugar
1½ cups milk
1½ tablespoons flour
2 tablespoons butter
3 egg yolks
4 egg whites
1 tablespoon confectioners' sugar (for sprinkling)

Soufflé dish (1 quart capacity)

Method

Prepare the soufflé dish with a paper collar and set oven at hot (425°F).

Rub half the cubes of sugar over the rind of the oranges until they are soaked with the zest (oil).

Mix 3 tablespoons of the milk with the flour to form a smooth paste. Scald remaining milk, add all the sugar cubes, cover pan and leave 5 minutes off the heat or until the sugar has dissolved. Return the pan to the heat, stir in the flour mixture gradually and bring to a boil, stirring. Boil 10 seconds, take from the heat and dot surface with butter. Cover and leave 5 minutes.

Stir to mix in the butter and beat in the egg yolks, one at a time. Beat the egg whites until they hold a stiff peak and, using a metal spoon, fold one-quarter into the warm orange mixture. Add the remaining egg white and fold together as lightly as possible.

Transfer the mixture to the prepared soufflé dish and bake at once in heated oven for 15–20 minutes or until the soufflé is puffed and brown. Remove the paper collar, sprinkle the top with confectioners' sugar and serve at once.

Lemon Soufflé

Make as for orange soufflé but finely grate the lemon rind instead of rubbing sugar cubes over it. Heat the grated rind and sugar with the milk and continue as for orange soufflé.

Soufflé Grand Marnier adds a touch of luxury to a menu

Soufflé Grand Marnier

1 large orange
8 sugar cubes
1 cup milk
3 eggs, separated
1½ tablespoons flour
1 tablespoon butter
2 egg whites
3 tablespoons sugar
3 tablespoons Grand Marnier
confectioners' sugar (for sprinkling)

Soufflé dish (1 quart capacity)

Method

Prepare the soufflé dish with a paper collar, butter the sides of the dish and collar and sprinkle with sugar, discarding the excess. Set oven at hot (425°F).

Rub sugar cubes over the rind of the orange until they are soaked with zest (oil). Heat milk gently with sugar cubes until dissolved.

Beat the egg yolks with the flour until smooth, stir in the hot milk, pour the mixture back into the pan and bring to a boil, stirring. Cook gently for 2 minutes, stirring constantly, then dot the top with butter, cover and let stand 5 minutes.

Stiffly whip the egg whites, add the sugar and beat 20 seconds longer or until the mixture is glossy. Stir the Grand Marnier into the orange mixture, then fold in one-quarter of the egg whites, using a metal spoon. Add the remaining egg white and fold together as lightly as possible.

Transfer the mixture to the prepared dish and bake at once in heated oven for 15–20 minutes or until the soufflé is puffed and brown. Remove the paper collar, sprinkle the top with confectioners' sugar and serve at once.

To prepare the soufflé partly in advance, make the orange mixture, dot with butter and let cool. Half an hour before serving, heat the orange mixture until hot to the touch and stir in the Grand Marnier. Stiffly whip the egg whites and continue as above.

SOUFFLE OMELETS

Soufflé omelets are usually served for dessert and can have a variety of fillings. The omelet mixture may be cooked in an omelet pan on top of the stove or in a soufflé or ovenproof dish in the oven.

Jam Omelet (Stove-top Method)

¼ cup apricot, strawberry or raspberry jam
4 large eggs, separated
1 tablespoon sugar
2 tablespoons light cream
1 tablespoon butter
2 tablespoons confectioners' sugar (for sprinkling)

2–3 metal skewers; 8 inch omelet pan

Alternative fillings for the omelet are fresh sliced strawberries mixed with 1 tablespoon warmed red currant jelly, or 2–3 bananas, sliced and sautéed in a little butter and then sprinkled generously with sugar and a little lemon juice.

Method

Beat the egg yolks with the sugar for at least 5 minutes until thick and light. Stir in the cream. Warm the jam in a small saucepan.

Beat the egg whites until they hold a stiff peak and fold into the yolk mixture with a metal spoon.

Set oven at hot (400°F) or turn on the broiler.

Heat the butter in an omelet pan and, when foaming, add the egg mixture. Spread it out in the pan and cook over moderate heat for 45–60 seconds to brown the bottom. Do not stir.

Put the pan in heated oven or under the broiler and cook 5 minutes or until the top is set. Spread omelet quickly with the warmed, melted jam, turn or slide onto a warm platter and fold over with a metal spatula.

Put the skewers in a flame or under broiler until red hot. (Heat several skewers at a time rather than one by one.)

Sprinkle the omelet with confectioners' sugar and mark a lattice across the top with the red hot skewers. Serve at once.

Note: marking soufflé omelets with heated skewers gives a traditional finish and a pleasant taste of caramel; otherwise, simply sprinkle the omelet with granulated instead of confectioners' sugar.

Rum Omelet

Make as for jam omelet and fill with jam or bananas. Then heat 2–3 tablespoons of rum, flame and pour around the finished omelet just before serving.

For jam omelet, spread the warm jam over cooked omelet

Slide the omelet off pan onto a warm plate and fold in half

Sprinkle the jam omelet with sugar and make a lattice pattern with hot skewers

Soufflé Omelet (Oven Method)

4 egg yolks
1 tablespoon butter
1½ tablespoons sugar
grated rind and juice of ½ lemon
5 egg whites
confectioners' sugar (for sprinkling)
¼ cup warmed and melted jam or fruit preserve

Oval ovenproof dish

Method

Set oven at moderately hot (375°F). Generously butter the ovenproof dish and sprinkle it with confectioners' sugar.

Beat the egg yolks with granulated sugar and lemon rind for 5 minutes or until thick and light. Stir in the lemon juice. Beat the egg whites until they hold a stiff peak and fold into the yolk mixture with a metal spoon.

Pour the mixture into the ovenproof dish and with a metal spatula make a hollow cavity down the center. Sprinkle with confectioners' sugar. Bake in heated oven for 7–10 minutes or until the omelet is puffed and lightly browned.

Spread the hollow of the omelet with jam or fruit preserve and serve at once.

Soufflé Rothschild

selection of fresh fruit – for example, 1 peach, 4 strawberries, 1 banana, 1 thin slice of pineapple
2 tablespoons rum, kirsch or Curaçao
3–4 tablespoons confectioners' sugar (for sprinkling)

For soufflé mixture
3 egg yolks
1 tablespoon sugar
¼ cup heavy cream, stiffly whipped
5 egg whites

Soufflé dish (1 quart capacity)

The basic mixture of this hot soufflé is similar to that of a soufflé omelet. Make it when there is plenty of fresh fruit available.

Method

Prepare the soufflé dish (without a paper collar) and set oven at hot (425°F).

Slice the fruit thinly, pour over the liqueur and sprinkle with 1 tablespoon of the confectioners' sugar or to taste. Cover and let stand 30 minutes. Drain and reserve the juice.

Beat the egg yolks with the sugar for at least 5 minutes until thick and light.

Watchpoint: the consistency of the finished soufflé depends on beating this mixture until it is really thick.

Stir in the cream with 2 tablespoons juice drained from the fruit. Beat the egg whites until they hold a stiff peak and, using a metal spoon, fold one-quarter into the egg yolk mixture. Add the remaining egg white and fold together as lightly as possible.

Spoon one-third of this mixture into the prepared soufflé dish, add half the drained fruit and cover with half the remaining soufflé mixture. Add the remaining fruit and soufflé mixture and bake in heated oven for 15–20 minutes or until the soufflé is well risen and browned.

Sprinkle the soufflé quickly with remaining confectioners' sugar and serve at once.

ROULADES

The type of soufflé called a roulade is cooked in a jelly roll pan or in a paper case. Then it is turned out, spread with a contrasting filling and rolled up like a jelly roll.

Spinach Roulade

¾ lb fresh or 1 package frozen spinach
1 tablespoon butter
salt and pepper
4 egg yolks
5 egg whites
3–4 tablespoons grated Parmesan cheese

For filling
2 cups (½ lb) mushrooms, thinly sliced
1 tablespoon butter
1 tablespoon flour
¾ cup milk
¼ teaspoon grated nutmeg
2–3 tablespoons light cream (optional)

15 X 10 inch jelly roll pan or roulade case

Method

Set oven at hot (400°F). Make the roulade case or line the pan with wax paper and grease it.

Wash and trim fresh spinach and cook in plenty of boiling salted water for 5 minutes or until tender (or cook frozen spinach according to package directions). Drain and press thoroughly to dry, chop coarsely and work through a sieve or food mill. Stir in butter, seasoning and egg yolks, one at a time. Alternatively, purée spinach in a blender with the butter, seasoning and egg yolks.

Beat egg whites until they hold a stiff peak and fold into the spinach mixture with a metal spoon. Spread quickly and evenly in the case or prepared pan and sprinkle with cheese. Bake at once in heated oven for 10 minutes or until the roulade is well risen and firm to the touch.

Meanwhile prepare the filling: sauté mushrooms in the butter until soft and stir in the flour off the heat with seasoning. Pour on the milk, bring mixture to a boil, stirring, and simmer until creamy. Take from heat, stir in the nutmeg and cream, if used, and season to taste.

Remove the cooked roulade from the oven, turn out onto a sheet of wax paper or foil and quickly peel off the paper. Trim off the sides, spread with mushroom filling and roll up like a jelly roll by tilting the paper underneath. Transfer to a hot platter. Serve at once.

How to make a Paper Roulade Case

1
To make a roulade case use either silicone paper or heavy duty foil. Cut a 17 X 12 inch rectangle and fold a 1 inch border, creasing it well

2
Cut a slit at each corner and fold one cut piece over the other to miter the corners

3
Fasten the corners with paper clips and slide the case onto a baking sheet. If using foil, brush lightly with melted butter or shortening before use

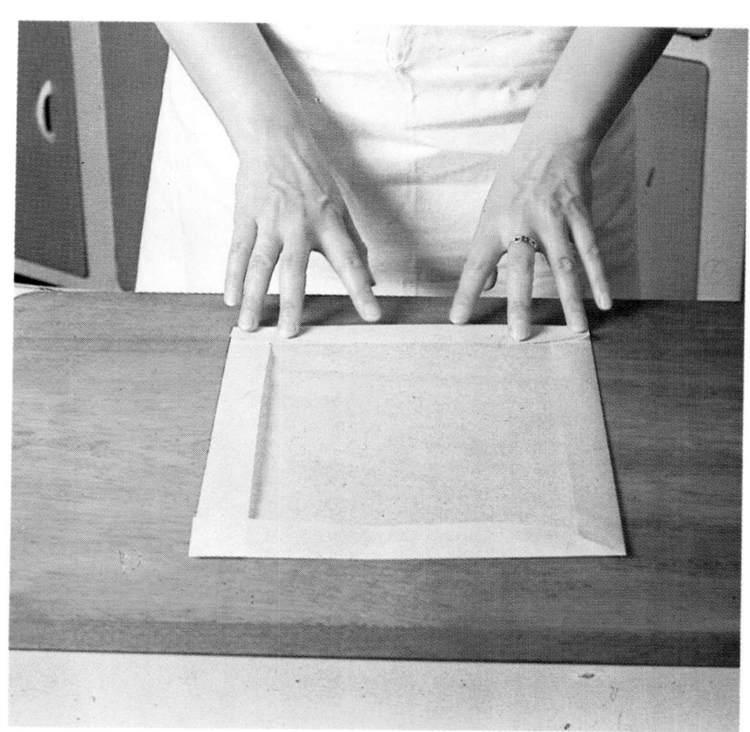

1

2

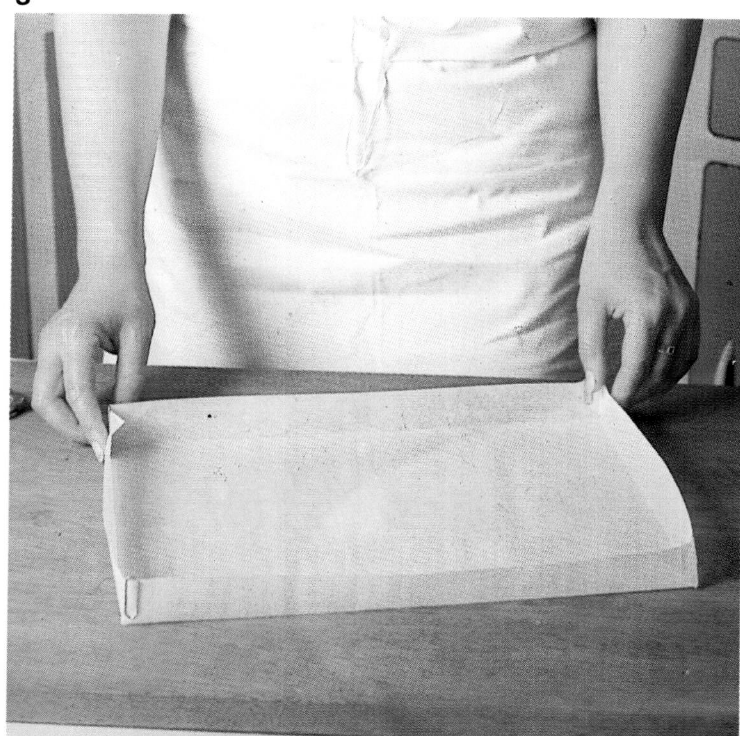

3

To make a fish roulade, stir $\frac{1}{4}$ cup sauce into the flaked fish; add the remaining sauce to the chopped hard-cooked eggs

Fold the egg whites into the fish mixture and spread it evenly over roulade case set on a baking sheet

Spread the filling over the cooked roulade, trim the sides, tilt the paper and roll up like a jelly roll

Salmon Roulade

1 cup ($\frac{1}{2}$ lb) flaked fresh cooked or canned salmon
4 eggs, separated
6 tablespoons grated Parmesan or dry sharp Cheddar cheese

For filling
2 cups béchamel sauce, made with 3 tablespoons butter, $2\frac{1}{2}$ tablespoons flour and 2 cups milk (infused with slice of onion, $\frac{1}{2}$ bay leaf, 6 peppercorns, blade of mace, few slices of carrot)
salt and pepper
1 teaspoon anchovy paste
3 hard-cooked eggs, finely chopped

15 X 10 inch jelly roll pan or roulade paper case

Tuna, crab meat or any cooked white fish can be substituted for the salmon.

Method

To make the filling: season the béchamel sauce well and add the anchovy paste. The sauce should be creamy and thick enough just to drop from the spoon.

Add $\frac{1}{4}$ cup of this sauce to the flaked salmon and stir remaining sauce into the chopped eggs. Cover and keep warm.

Make the roulade case or grease the jelly roll pan, line it with wax paper and grease again. Set oven at hot (400°F).

Beat the egg yolks, one at a time, into the fish mixture with 2 tablespoons cheese. Beat egg whites until they hold a stiff peak and fold them into the fish mixture with a metal spoon. Spread quickly and evenly in the case or prepared pan and bake at once in heated oven for 10–15 minutes or until the roulade is well risen and firm to the touch.

Have a large sheet of wax paper or foil sprinkled with the remaining cheese ready. Quickly turn the roulade onto this and peel off the cooking paper at once. Trim off the sides, spread with the egg filling, tilt paper and roll up like a jelly roll. Transfer to a hot platter and sprinkle with more cheese, if you like. Serve at once.

Hot soufflés, soufflé omelets and roulades

Fish roulade is filled with chopped hard-cooked eggs and sprinkled with grated cheese

BUFFET DINNER FOR A DOZEN

A buffet dinner for 12 is easy if you choose dishes that can be prepared in advance like ham cornets or a rich egg mousse. The suggested salads will stand up well and the flavors of the meringue vacherin filled with chestnuts will blend all the more happily if left an hour or two before serving.

Pouilly Fumé and Fumé Blanc are remarkably clean, dry, fresh-tasting white wines, made from the same grape – sauvignon blanc – on both sides of the Atlantic. The Loire wine should not be confused with Pouilly Fuissé from Burgundy; it has a splendid bouquet and should be an ideal foil for the cold meats in this menu. The California version is equally good, although perhaps somewhat harder to find.

Spicy Tomato Soup

Egg Mousse *Ham Cornets*
Platters of Cold Cooked Meats

Various Salads

Tarte aux Pruneaux (Prune Flan)
or
Vacherin aux Marrons
(Meringue with Chestnut Purée)

White wine – Pouilly Fumé (Loire)
or Fumé Blanc (California)

TIMETABLE

1–2 days before
For egg mousse: make mayonnaise very thick so that it can be thinned as needed. Store in covered jar in refrigerator. Prepare béchamel sauce and cover with plastic wrap to prevent a skin from forming while cooling. When cold, beat well and store in covered container in refrigerator.
Make devil sauce for egg mousse and store in tightly capped bottle or jar in refrigerator.
For ham cornets: prepare aspic, store in airtight container and refrigerate.
For salads: make vinaigrette dressing and store in tightly capped bottle or jar. Shake to mix before using.
For vacherin: bake meringue rounds and store in airtight containers. Prepare chestnut filling and store in covered container in refrigerator.
For tarte aux pruneaux: prepare almond pastry dough, wrap in plastic bag and refrigerate.

Day before
Make egg mousse, cover tightly and chill.
Make spicy tomato soup.
Bake ham (see Volume 7) and roast turkey (see Volume 8). Cool, cover tightly and store in refrigerator.
Bake almond flan shell and store in airtight container.
Make almond filling for prunes. Cook prunes and stuff them. Make red currant jelly glaze.

Morning of party
Make ham cornets. Prepare garnishes for mousse and store in plastic bag or cover with plastic wrap and chill.
Prepare all salads, cover and chill.
Make custard for flan, fill and complete it; cover and refrigerate.

1 hour before party
Carve turkey and ham and cover with plastic wrap to keep moist.
Unmold mousse and ham cornets, garnish them, cover and chill.
Complete all salads without adding dressing. Refrigerate until serving.
Whip cream, finish and arrange the vacherin aux marrons on serving tray.
Place tarte aux pruneaux on platter.

Just before serving
Reheat soup and add port.
Add dressings to salads.

You will find that **cooking times** given in the individual recipes for these dishes have sometimes been adapted in the timetable to help you when cooking and serving this menu as a party meal.

Spicy Tomato Soup

4 cups (2 lb) canned tomatoes
2 tablespoons butter
2 onions, finely sliced
1 tablespoon flour
1 teaspoon paprika
1 tablespoon tomato paste
2 quarts chicken or turkey stock (made from giblets)
salt and pepper
bouquet garni
blade of mace
1 clove
2 tablespoons rice (optional)
$\frac{1}{4}$ cup port (optional)

Method
In a kettle melt the butter, add the onion and cook gently until soft but not browned. Stir in the flour, paprika and tomato paste. Add tomatoes and crush them well with a spoon. Pour on the stock, add seasoning, with bouquet garni and spices tied in a piece of cheesecloth, and stir until boiling. Simmer 30 minutes, remove cheesecloth bag and work the soup through a sieve or purée it in a blender.

Return soup to a pan with the rice, if used, and simmer 10–12 minutes or until the rice is cooked. Taste for seasoning.

Just before serving, reheat the soup and stir in the port, if you like.

Quantities
This buffet menu serves 12 people.

Egg Mousse

12 hard-cooked eggs, chopped
$1\frac{1}{2}$ cups mayonnaise (see page 21)
2 envelopes gelatin
1 cup chicken stock or white wine
béchamel sauce, made with 3 tablespoons butter, 3 tablespoons flour and 2 cups milk (infused with a slice of onion, 6 peppercorns, blade of mace and bay leaf)
salt and pepper
pinch of cayenne (or to taste)
$\frac{1}{2}$ teaspoon Worcestershire sauce (or to taste)
$\frac{1}{2}$ teaspoon anchovy paste (or to taste)
1 cup heavy cream, whipped until it holds a soft shape

For devil sauce
2 cups (1 lb) canned tomatoes
1 teaspoon sugar
1–2 cloves of garlic, crushed (or to taste)
$\frac{1}{4}$ cup oil
1 tablespoon vinegar
2 tablespoons Worcestershire sauce
2 tablespoons ketchup
1 tablespoon dry mustard

To garnish
sliced tomatoes or cucumber, lettuce hearts, or watercress (see right)

Soufflé dish or charlotte mold ($2\frac{1}{2}$ quart capacity)

Method
Lightly oil the soufflé dish or mold.

Combine the chopped eggs in a bowl with the mayonnaise.

In a small pan sprinkle the gelatin over the cold chicken stock or wine and stand 5 minutes until spongy. Set over a pan of hot water until the gelatin has dissolved, then stir it into the béchamel sauce.

Thin cucumber slices are one of the suggested garnishes for rich egg mousse

Add to the egg mixture and season well with salt, cayenne, Worcestershire sauce and anchovy paste, adding more if you like.

Cool the mixture and when it starts to thicken fold in the whipped cream. Spoon the mixture into the prepared soufflé dish or mold and chill 2 hours or more until set.

To prepare the devil sauce: combine all the ingredients, adding more seasoning to taste; pour into a sauce boat.

To serve, run a small knife around the edge of the mousse, pull the mixture away from the dish or mold at one side to break the airlock and carefully turn out the mousse onto a platter. Add the garnish. Serve the sauce separately.

Suggested Egg Mousse Garnishes

Cucumber. Wipe the cucumber and slice it thinly. Make a cut in each slice from the center to the edge. Twist one cut edge away from the center to make the slices stand up.

Tomato. Peel the tomatoes, core them, slice thinly and place, overlapping, around the base of the mousse. Garnish the top with a small bunch of watercress and a few more slices of tomato.

Lettuce hearts. Wash and chill Bibb lettuces or hearts of Boston lettuces until crisp, then cut in quarters. Arrange them around the base of the mousse; garnish the top with cucumber slices and 1–2 sprigs of watercress.

Watercress. Wash and trim sprigs of watercress. Arrange a small bunch on top of the mousse. Circle the base with additional sprigs.

Set the filled ham cornets on a bed of chopped aspic and garnish with watercress

Line the cornet molds with ham slices, then set the molds upright in an egg box

Pipe the pâté de foie mousse mixture into the ham cones

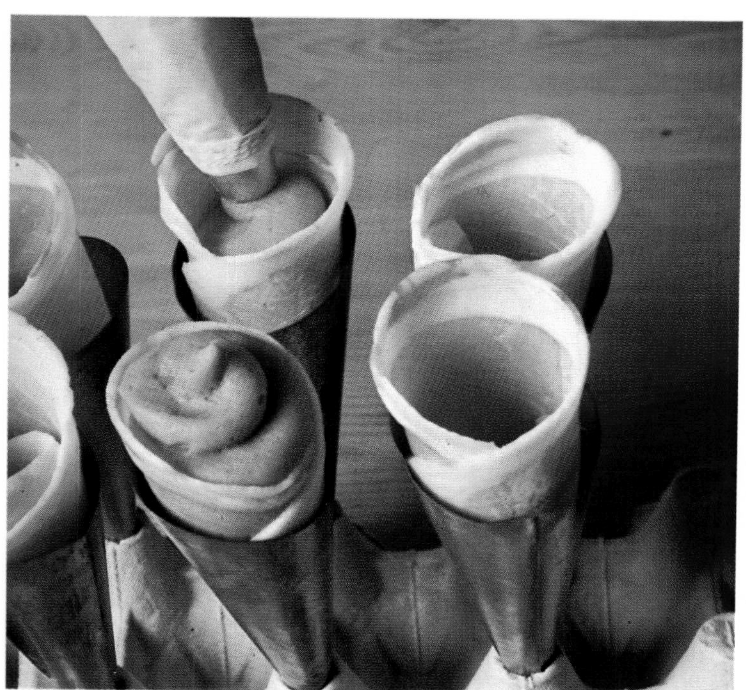

Ham Cornets

12 thin slices of cooked ham
4 cups aspic, cool but still liquid

For mousse filling
2 cans (4 oz each) pâté de foie
1 tablespoon butter, softened
béchamel sauce, made with
2 tablespoons butter,
2 tablespoons flour and 1 cup milk (infused with slice of onion, 6 peppercorns, blade of mace and bay leaf)
salt and pepper
1 tablespoon sherry
½ teaspoon Dijon-style mustard
¼ cup heavy cream, stiffly whipped

For garnish
12 small mushrooms (cooked in a little water and a squeeze of lemon juice) or 12 thin slices of canned truffle
bunch of watercress

12 cornet molds; pastry bag and ¼ inch plain tube

Method

Make the béchamel sauce and let cool. Trim slices of ham, if necessary, and line the cornet molds with them. Set molds upright in an egg box.

To make the filling: beat the pâté de foie and softened butter together in a bowl. Beat in the cold béchamel sauce, season with salt and pepper, add sherry and mustard and mix thoroughly. Fold in the whipped cream. Spoon mousse mixture into the pastry bag fitted with the plain tube and pipe it into the ham cornets to fill them. Top with a cooked mushroom or a slice of truffle and chill at least 1 hour until firm.

Pour about three-quarters of the aspic into a shallow baking pan. Chill in the refrigerator until set.

Remove ham cornets from the molds and set on a wire rack. Place the remaining aspic in a container in a pan of ice water. As soon as it begins to thicken, spoon or brush it over the cornets.

Turn out the firm layer of aspic from the baking pan onto a wet sheet of brown paper and chop it coarsely with a wet knife. Arrange a layer of it on a platter. Set the cornets on top, cover and chill. Just before serving, garnish with watercress.

Quick Aspic

For 4 cups: put 1 can consommé in a pan, sprinkle 1½ envelopes gelatin over it, let stand 5 minutes until spongy and dissolve over a pan of hot water. Stir in 2 more cans of consommé and, if you like, 2–3 tablespoons sherry or brandy.

For homemade aspic, refer to savory and sweet gelatins in Volume 8.

Platters of Cold Cooked Meats

Some of your guests may prefer foods less rich than ham cornets and egg mousse, so serve platters of cold cooked meats such as ham and turkey.

Various Salads

You will need at least 3 salads for your buffet. A good combination would be cauliflower with mustard mayonnaise for a piquant touch, celery, apple and walnut for a crunchy texture, and a creamy potato salad. Recipes are in Volume 6.

Tarte aux Pruneaux
(Prune Flan)

3 cups (1 lb) large prunes
1 cup red wine
¼ cup red currant jelly glaze

For almond pastry
¼ cup whole blanched almonds, ground
1½ cups flour
½ cup butter
⅓ cup sugar
1 egg yolk
1–2 tablespoons cold water

For custard
1½ cups milk
2 egg yolks
¼ cup sugar
1½ tablespoons cornstarch
1 teaspoon vanilla
1 cup heavy cream, stiffly whipped

For almond filling
½ cup whole blanched almonds, ground
½ cup sugar
½–1 egg white, beaten until frothy

8–9 inch flan ring

Serves 6 people.

Method

Soak the prunes in the wine for 2–3 hours.

Prepare the dough like pie pastry, adding the almonds and sugar after rubbing in the butter and before mixing with the egg yolk and enough water to make a smooth dough. Chill 30 minutes.

Set oven at moderately hot (375°F). Roll out the dough and line flan ring. Bake blind in heated oven for 20–25 minutes or until the pastry is brown. Cool on a wire rack.

Simmer the prunes in the wine until tender.

Watchpoint: cook the prunes very gently in a pan with a tight-fitting lid to avoid evaporation because there is so little liquid.

Lift the prunes from the pan with a slotted spoon and let cool. Add red currant jelly to the wine to make a glaze. Melt the jelly over low heat, stirring until smooth; strain the glaze.

To make the custard: scald the milk. In a bowl beat egg yolks and sugar until thick and light in color and stir in cornstarch. Stir in hot milk, return mixture to pan and cook, stirring, until custard thickens. Simmer 1 minute, take from heat, add vanilla and cool. Fold in whipped cream and spread in flan shell.

Slit the prunes down one side and remove the pits.

To make the filling: mix the almonds and sugar and add just enough egg white to bind the mixture. Stuff into the prunes. Arrange prunes on top of custard filling. Warm red currant jelly glaze, if necessary, and brush or spoon over prunes. Chill before serving.

Remove the pits and fill prunes neatly with almond mixture

Arrange stuffed prunes on top of the custard-filled flan shell

Tarte aux pruneaux, made with almond-stuffed prunes, is a delicious dessert

Vacherin aux Marrons
(Meringue Rounds with Chestnut Purée)

For meringue
4 egg whites
1 cup sugar

For filling
1 lb fresh chestnuts, skinned (see page 90) or 2½ cups canned chestnuts, drained
1 vanilla bean or 1 teaspoon vanilla extract
2 tablespoons sugar
¼ cup water
1 cup heavy cream, stiffly whipped

To decorate
confectioners' sugar
1 square (1 oz) semisweet chocolate, grated

Pastry bag; ½ inch plain tube and medium star tube

Serves 6 people.

Method
Set oven at low (275°F). Line 2 baking sheets with silicone paper.

To make meringue: beat egg whites in a bowl until they hold a stiff peak, add 1 tablespoon of the measured sugar and beat for 1 minute or until mixture is glossy. Gradually fold in the remaining sugar with a metal spoon. Divide meringue mixture in half and spread it carefully onto the 2 prepared baking sheets in circles 8–9 inches in diameter or use a pastry bag fitted with the plain tube and pipe meringue in a spiral pattern.

Bake meringue rounds in heated oven for 50–60 minutes or until they are dry and very lightly browned. Cool on a wire rack and when almost cold peel off the paper.

Almost cover the fresh chestnuts with water and simmer, covered, with the vanilla bean, if using, until tender. Drain, discard vanilla bean and work chestnuts through a sieve; if using canned chestnuts, work them through a sieve also.

In a small pan dissolve the sugar in water and bring to a boil. Cool and beat the sugar syrup into the chestnut purée; add vanilla extract, if using. If you like, the cooked fresh or canned chestnuts can be puréed in a blender with the sugar syrup.

Mix half the whipped cream with chestnut purée and sandwich the meringue rounds. Sprinkle the top with confectioners' sugar and grated chocolate. Pipe remaining cream on top in rosettes, using the pastry bag fitted with the star tube.

Pipe two large rounds of meringue on the silicone paper

Sandwich the baked meringue rounds with chestnut purée

Vacherin aux marrons is decorated with rosettes of whipped cream

Boiled beef with dumplings makes a hearty family meal

COLD-WEATHER DISHES

When the weather is near freezing, few dishes are more welcome than such hearty favorites as boiled beef with dumplings, bacon and sauerkraut, and upside-down gingerbread. The list is long and familiar – reminiscent of schooldays and large family gatherings.

Boiled Beef with Dumplings

3–4 lb corned brisket of beef
3–4 onions
3–4 carrots, quartered
1 small cabbage, quartered
salt and pepper

For dumplings
2 cups self-rising flour
$\frac{1}{2}$ cup beef suet, chopped or ground
about $\frac{3}{4}$ cup water

Beef suet is available at some supermarkets and from butchers.

Method
Place the beef in a large kettle, cover with cold water and bring slowly to a boil.

Watchpoint: keep the liquid well skimmed of fat while bringing to a boil. A spoonful or two of cold water added during boiling will help to bring the scum to the surface. This, combined with gentle simmering, will keep the cooking liquid clear – an especially important step if the liquid is to be used later for soup.

Cover pan and simmer the beef, allowing 25–30 minutes per lb. Add the onion and carrot $1\frac{1}{2}$ hours before the end of cooking, and the quartered cabbage 35–45 minutes before the end of cooking.

To make the dumplings: mix the flour, suet and 1 teaspoon salt together. Add enough water to make a fairly firm dough, divide this into walnut-sized pieces and roll lightly in a little flour. About 20–30 minutes before the end of cooking time, float the dumplings in the pan with the beef. Keep covered and simmer until the dumplings are light and tender. Turn them once during cooking.

Watchpoint: when adding the dumplings, make sure they have plenty of room to swell. If the pan is very full, it is better to cook them separately in stock or salted water.

To serve, lift out the dumplings with a slotted spoon and arrange around a large hot platter with the vegetables. Set the beef in the center, taste the cooking liquid for seasoning and serve some in a sauce boat as a separate gravy. Serve with sauerkraut salad, if you like.

Fresh or corned beef may be used for boiling. Both types of beef are cooked in the same way and are often served with vegetables added during cooking. However, some recipes call for vegetables to be added at the beginning of cooking. By this method all their flavor is extracted and they should be discarded before serving.

The French reduce the cooking liquid by boiling until it is well flavored, then serve it as a gravy with the beef. It may also be used as a base for consommé or broth.

Alternatively, the liquid can be served as a soup before the beef, usually with a slice of toasted bread added to the bowl.

Bacon with Frankfurters and Sauerkraut

1 lb lean bacon, in the piece
4 cups (2 lb) fresh or canned sauerkraut
1 carrot
1 medium onion, stuck with 1 clove
2–3 tablespoons dry white wine, stock or water
salt and pepper
kneaded butter, made with 2 tablespoons butter and 1 tablespoon flour

For garnish
10–12 small potatoes
8 frankfurters
1 tablespoon parsley

Method
Put the bacon in a pan, cover with cold water, bring slowly to a boil, cover and simmer gently for about 1 hour. Leave to cool in the liquid.

Prepare the sauerkraut (see box); arrange it in a casserole with the carrot and onion. Put the bacon on top, add the wine, stock or water, season and cover with buttered foil.

Cover the pot with a tight-fitting lid and bake in a moderate oven (350°F) for about $1\frac{1}{2}$ hours or until the bacon is tender and the liquid has evaporated.

Cook the potatoes in boiling salted water for 12–15 minutes or until tender, drain and keep warm. Poach the frankfurters in water that is almost simmering for 10–12 minutes and leave in the water to keep hot.

Take out the bacon and keep warm. Discard the carrot and onion with the clove, or if you like, slice the carrot and onion, discarding the clove, and stir into the sauerkraut.

Add kneaded butter to the pan in small pieces; heat, stirring, for 2–3 minutes and keep warm. Slice the bacon.

Arrange the sauerkraut in a serving dish and place the bacon slices, overlapping, on top. Place potatoes at either end of the dish with the drained frankfurters, halved if you like, on top of the bacon slices. Sprinkle the potatoes with chopped parsley.

Sauerkraut Salad

2 cups (1 lb) fresh or canned sauerkraut
1 green pepper, finely chopped
1 small onion, finely chopped
2 stalks of celery, finely chopped
1 cup chili sauce
$\frac{1}{3}$ cup brown sugar
3 tablespoons lemon juice

Method
Prepare the sauerkraut (see below) and place in a salad bowl. Stir in the green pepper, onion and celery. Combine the chili sauce, brown sugar and lemon juice. Pour onto the salad and toss well.

Sauerkraut literally means sour or fermented cabbage. It is made by shredding white, firm cabbage, then leaving it for 4–6 weeks to ferment in brine.

Sauerkraut is sold fresh in some delicatessens and it also comes in cans.

Fresh sauerkraut should be drained and soaked in cold water for about 15 minutes before cooking. Canned sauerkraut may be washed to remove the salty taste before cooking; squeeze out water with hands or between 2 plates.

Bacon, frankfurters and sauerkraut are a popular combination

Spoon the tomato sauce over the browned bitki before baking them

Bitki

$1\frac{1}{2}$ lb ground beef (not too lean)
1 large onion, finely chopped
$1\frac{1}{2}$ tablespoons chopped parsley
6 slices of white bread, crusts removed
about 1 cup cold water
salt and pepper
flour (for sprinkling)
$\frac{1}{4}$ cup oil
2–3 cups tomato sauce
$\frac{3}{4}$ cup sour cream or plain yogurt

Method

Put the beef in a bowl with the onion and parsley. Cut the bread in pieces and cover with cold water. Leave until thoroughly soaked, then squeeze as dry as possible. Break into coarse crumbs with 2 forks, then mix into the meat.

Work the beef mixture thoroughly, gradually adding about 1 cup cold water and plenty of seasoning. When smooth and light in consistency, shape mixture into $2\frac{1}{2}$ inch cakes about $\frac{3}{4}$ inch thick. Sprinkle them with flour on both sides.

In a skillet heat the oil and brown the cakes on both sides. Arrange in an ovenproof dish, pour over the tomato sauce and bake in a moderate oven (350°F) for 30 minutes.

Spoon over the sour cream or yogurt just before serving and return to the oven for a few minutes to reheat. Serve with buttered noodles or spätzle.

Spätzle

3 cups flour
salt
2 eggs, beaten to mix
1 cup water

For serving
$\frac{1}{2}$ cup melted butter
pepper

Method

Put the flour and $\frac{1}{2}$ teaspoon salt in a bowl, make a well in the center and add eggs and water. Stir and work to a smooth soft dough, adding a little more flour or water if necessary. Divide the dough in half and press out thinly on a floured board. Have a large pan of boiling salted water ready.

Cut thin slivers of dough with a knife (wet the knife to prevent it from sticking) and drop them into boiling water. Simmer gently for 5–7 minutes or until the spätzle rise to the surface. Lift them out with a slotted spoon and keep in a warm place in a pan with melted butter.

Cook the remaining spätzle in the same way, adding them to the butter and heat thoroughly with plenty of pepper and a little salt if needed.

Spätzle may be served when still tender and white or they may be fried in the butter until golden.

Braised Short Ribs of Beef

3–$3\frac{1}{2}$ lb short ribs of beef, cut in large pieces
2 tablespoons oil
2 onions, coarsely chopped
2 carrots, cut in cubes
2 stalks of celery, sliced
1 teaspoon tomato paste
1 clove of garlic, crushed
1 cup red wine
1 cup beef stock
bouquet garni
kneaded butter, made with $1\frac{1}{2}$ tablespoons butter and 2 teaspoons flour
salt and pepper

Method

In a flameproof casserole heat the oil and brown the ribs on all sides. Remove them, add the onion, carrot and celery, turn down heat, cover and cook gently for 5–7 minutes.

Stir in the tomato paste and add the garlic, wine, stock and bouquet garni. Bring to a boil and cook until the liquid is reduced by one-third.

Put back the ribs, cover the pot and braise in a moderate oven (350°F) for $1\frac{1}{2}$ hours or until the ribs are very tender.

Take the ribs out, arrange them on a hot platter and keep warm. Strain the gravy and reheat. Whisk in kneaded butter, a little at a time to thicken the gravy, and taste for seasoning.

Spoon a little gravy over the ribs and serve the rest separately. Serve with mashed potatoes and braised Belgian endive.

Braised Belgian Endive

6–8 medium heads of Belgian endive
2 tablespoons butter
juice of $\frac{1}{2}$ lemon
$\frac{1}{2}$ teaspoon salt, dissolved in 1 tablespoon water
black pepper, freshly ground

Method

Wipe the endive, remove any wilted outer leaves and scoop out the small core at the base with a vegetable peeler.

Rub butter around a casserole, put in the endive and pour over the lemon juice and salt water. Sprinkle with pepper, cover with buttered foil and add the lid. Bake in a moderate oven (350°F) for 1 hour or until the endive is very tender.

Ham and Pease Pudding

3–4 lb piece of country ham, on the bone
2 onions, quartered
2 carrots, quartered
2–3 stalks of celery, cut in half
6 peppercorns

For pease pudding
2 cups (1 lb) dried split peas
2 tablespoons butter
1 egg, beaten to mix
salt and pepper

Method

Soak the ham and peas in separate bowls overnight in water to cover. Drain.

Place the ham in a kettle, cover with cold water, bring to a boil slowly and skim thoroughly. Add the onion, carrot, celery and peppercorns, cover and simmer $1\frac{1}{2}$–2 hours (30 minutes per lb) or until the ham is tender.

To make pease pudding: cover peas with cold salted water, add the lid, bring to a boil and simmer $1\frac{1}{2}$ hours or until tender, adding more water if it reduces too much. Drain and work the peas through a sieve or food mill or purée them in a blender. Beat in the butter and egg and season well.

Line a bowl with cheesecloth, spoon the pease mixture into it and tie up in a ball. Add the cheesecloth ball to the ham for the last 35–45 minutes cooking.

To serve, drain the ham, remove any skin and set ham on a platter. Untie the cheesecloth, turn out the ball of pease pudding on a separate platter and serve.

Note: an alternative way to make pease pudding is to tie the soaked peas in cheesecloth, leaving room for expansion, and simmer them in the cheesecloth for $1\frac{1}{2}$ hours. When tender, turn out, purée them, add butter, egg and seasoning and finish cooking as before.

Pease pudding is the pease 'porridge' described in the nursery rhyme:

Pease porridge hot,
Pease porridge cold,
Pease porridge in
the pot,
Nine days old.

Hot Pot

4–6 shoulder lamb chops
4 lambs' kidneys
5 medium potatoes, sliced
3 large onions, thinly sliced
1 cup ($\frac{1}{4}$ lb) large mushrooms, quartered
2 tablespoons beef drippings or shortening
salt and pepper
2–$2\frac{1}{2}$ cups well-flavored beef stock

Method

Trim excess fat from the chops. Skin kidneys, pull out and cut away as much core as possible. Cut kidneys in half and remove rest of core.

Spread a large casserole generously with beef drippings or shortening. Arrange a generous layer of potato slices in the bottom and sprinkle with onion. Put the chops on top, season and lay the halved kidneys with mushrooms on top. Cover with remaining potatoes, arranging the top layer in a neat pattern. Dot with remaining drippings or shortening and pour in 2 cups stock at the side of the casserole.

Cover and bake in a moderate oven (350°F) for 30 minutes. Lower heat to moderately low (325°F) and bake $1\frac{1}{2}$ hours longer. Then remove lid, raise heat again to 350°F and bake until the potatoes are well browned. If the dish seems dry during cooking, add a little more stock.

Lamb and Potato Casserole

$2\frac{1}{2}$–3 lb boned shoulder of lamb, with the bones
4 large potatoes
seasoned flour, made with 1 teaspoon salt and pinch of pepper
3 tablespoons oil
2 large onions, finely chopped
1 tablespoon tomato paste
$1\frac{1}{2}$–2 cups stock
salt and pepper
2 cups ($\frac{1}{2}$ lb) mushrooms, quartered
3 tablespoons melted butter
$\frac{1}{4}$ cup grated Parmesan cheese (for sprinkling)

Method

Cut the lamb in 1–$1\frac{1}{2}$ inch cubes, discarding any fat, and make the stock with the bone. Toss the cubes with seasoned flour to coat well. Set the oven at moderately low (325°F).

In a large flameproof casserole heat the oil until hot, add the cubes of lamb and fry a few pieces at a time, until all are golden brown.

Watchpoint: do not put in more meat than will cover the bottom of the pot or the lamb will stew instead of frying quickly.

When all the lamb is browned, remove it and reserve; add the onion, lower heat, cover and cook until the onion is soft, shaking the pot and stirring from time to time. Stir in the tomato paste and $1\frac{1}{2}$ cups stock and bring to a boil. Put back the lamb, add a little extra seasoning, if needed, cover the pot tightly and cook in heated oven for $1\frac{1}{2}$–2 hours or until the lamb is tender. Add more stock if the pot gets dry. Add the mushrooms to the pot 15 minutes before the end of cooking.

If not serving immediately,

spread the lamb and mushroom mixture in shallow ovenproof dishes to cook, then cover and chill.

To finish: scrub the potatoes and cook them in their skins in boiling water for 15–20 minutes or until tender. Peel them while still hot, holding them in a dish towel, and cut them into ½ inch slices. Arrange these, overlapping, on top of the lamb mixture and brush them with melted butter. Sprinkle with grated Parmesan cheese and bake in a moderately hot oven (375°F) for 30 minutes or until the potatoes are brown and crisp.

Tomato Coulis

3 cups (1½ lb) canned tomatoes, crushed
1 clove of garlic, crushed
salt and pepper
1 teaspoon sugar
¾ cup cooking liquid (from the lamb)

Method

Put all the ingredients in a pan and simmer, stirring occasionally, until the mixture is thick and pulpy. Taste for seasoning and serve.

Stuffed Breast of Lamb Dundee

3–3½ lb breast of lamb, on the bone
1 onion, stuck with 1 clove
1 carrot
salt
6 peppercorns
bouquet garni, including 1 stalk of celery
2 tablespoons red wine vinegar
¼ cup butter
3 medium onions, sliced and blanched
½ cup fresh white breadcrumbs
½ cup grated sharp Cheddar cheese

Method

Put the lamb in a large kettle with cold water to cover, bring to a boil and skim well. Add the whole onion and carrot, salt and peppercorns, bouquet garni and wine vinegar and simmer gently for 1½ hours or until tender.

Take the meat from the pan, remove all the bones, then press the meat between 2 boards or plates until cold. Strain and reserve the cooking liquid.

In a pan melt the butter, add the blanched onions and cook gently in butter until golden. Place the lamb in a shallow ovenproof dish, cover with the onions and top with the breadcrumbs and cheese, mixed together. Spoon any butter left from the onions on top and pour around about ¾ cup of the reserved cooking liquid. Bake in a hot oven (400°F) for about 30 minutes or until lamb is brown and crisp.

Serve with mashed potatoes and tomato coulis.

Brunswick Stew

3–3½ lb chicken, cut in pieces
1 lb shin of beef, on the bone, cut in pieces
1 ham bone (from a country ham)
1 squirrel, cut in pieces (optional)
6 cups water
¼ cup sugar
bouquet garni
1 onion, sliced
3 tomatoes, peeled, seeded and chopped or 2 cups canned tomatoes, chopped
1 cup chopped celery
1 cup fresh or frozen lima beans
2 large potatoes
2 cups fresh or frozen corn kernels
¼ cup butter
1 teaspoon dried crushed red pepper
salt and pepper

Method

In a large kettle put the chicken pieces, beef, ham bone, squirrel if used, water, sugar and bouquet garni. Bring to a boil and skim well. Cover and simmer gently for 1 hour or until the chicken and squirrel are tender. Take them out and add the onion, tomatoes, celery and beans. Continue simmering for 20–30 minutes or until the beans are tender, stirring often.

While the stew is simmering, cook the potatoes in plenty of boiling salted water for 15–20 minutes or until tender. Drain and work them through a sieve or ricer.

Remove the ham bone, take out the beef and pull all meat from the bones – it should come away easily. Put the meat back in the stew and add the corn. Simmer 10 minutes, then add the butter, red pepper and seasoning to taste and heat until the butter is melted.

Stir the sieved potato into the stew. Put back the chicken and squirrel and cook the stew, stirring often, for 15 minutes or until it is soft enough to be eaten with a spoon. Remove bouquet garni and serve.

Brunswick County in North Carolina, and in Virginia, both take credit for having invented Brunswick stew. One thing is certain, however. The stew uses local southern ingredients and has long been a favorite dish at political rallies, church suppers and other large gatherings. Today, the traditional basic ingredient of squirrel has largely been replaced by chicken but here we give you a recipe that uses both.

Broadway Chicken Pie

3–3$\frac{1}{2}$ lb roasting chicken
2 cup quantity of flaky pastry, chilled (see right)
1 onion, finely chopped
$\frac{1}{4}$ cup butter
$\frac{1}{4}$ cup rice, boiled
1 package frozen chopped spinach, thawed
1 egg, beaten to mix
salt and pepper
1$\frac{1}{2}$ cups stock (made from chicken bones and giblets)
$\frac{1}{4}$ cup Madeira or sherry
kneaded butter, made with 1 tablespoon butter and $\frac{1}{2}$ tablespoon flour
6 slices of bacon, fried until crisp and drained
2 cups ($\frac{1}{2}$ lb) mushrooms, whole or quartered
2 tomatoes, peeled, seeded and cut in wedges
1 egg beaten with $\frac{1}{2}$ tablespoon salt (for glaze)

Baking dish (2 quart capacity); trussing needle and string

Method

Bone the chicken, lay it, skin side down, on a board.

Sauté the onion in 2 tablespoons butter until soft but not browned, and add to the rice and spinach. Add 1 beaten egg and seasoning, spread the mixture on the chicken and sew it up with a trussing needle and string.

Set oven at moderate (350°F).

In a flameproof casserole heat the remaining butter and brown the chicken on all sides. Add the stock, cover and braise in the heated oven for 50–60 minutes or until a skewer inserted in the center for 1 minute is hot to the touch when withdrawn.

Take out the chicken and boil the stock to reduce it to 1 cup. Add the Madeira or sherry and whisk in the kneaded butter, a few pieces at a time, until the sauce thickens. Simmer 1–2 minutes and taste for seasoning.

Cut the chicken into $\frac{3}{8}$ inch slices and arrange in layers in the baking dish with the bacon, mushrooms and tomatoes; spoon over the sauce and cool.

Roll out the pastry dough, cover the pie, brush with egg glaze and decorate the top with pastry leaves. Chill 30 minutes, then bake in a hot oven (400°F) for 30–35 minutes or until the pastry is crisp and brown.

Flaky Pastry

2 cups flour
pinch of salt
6 tablespoons butter
6 tablespoons shortening or lard
8–10 tablespoons ice water

Method

Sift the flour with the salt into a bowl. Divide the fats into 4 portions (two of butter, two of shortening or lard and use alternatively); rub one portion, butter or shortening, with the fingertips into the flour and mix with enough cold water to make a firm dough. The amount of water varies with different flours, but an average quantity for 2 cups flour is just over $\frac{1}{2}$ cup or 8–10 tablespoons. The more finely ground the flour, the more water it will absorb.

Knead dough lightly until smooth, then roll out to a rectangle about 6 X 15 inches. Put a second portion of fat (not the same kind as the first portion rubbed in), cut in small pieces, onto two-thirds of the dough. Fold in three, put in a cloth or plastic wrap and chill 15 minutes. Place dough so that open edge is towards you, roll out again to a rectangle. Put on a third portion of fat in pieces, fold dough in three, put in a cloth or plastic wrap and refrigerate 15 minutes.

Roll out the dough again, put on the remaining fat, cut in pieces, roll and fold as before. If the dough looks streaky, give one more turn and roll out and fold. If wrapped in an airtight plastic bag, dough keeps up to 1 week in the refrigerator, or for several weeks in the freezer.

Shrimp and Oyster Gumbo

$\frac{3}{4}$ lb uncooked peeled shrimps
1 cup oysters, shucked, with their liquor
2 tablespoons lard
$\frac{3}{4}$ cup (6 oz) chopped, cooked country or Virginia ham
1 lb okra, sliced
2 onions, finely chopped
salt
pinch of cayenne or $\frac{1}{4}$ dried red pepper pod
boiled rice (for serving)

Method

In a heavy-based pan melt the lard and fry the shrimps for 2–3 minutes or until they turn bright red. Take them out and reserve.

Add the ham and brown it. Stir in the okra and onions with salt and cayenne or red pepper, cover and cook gently for 15 minutes.

Drain the oysters, reserving their liquor, and add enough water to the liquor to make 2 cups. Add this oyster liquor to the pan, cover and continue simmering for 1 hour – if the mixture becomes very thick, add more water. Add the shrimps and simmer 30 minutes longer. Add the oysters and simmer 10 minutes or just until the edges curl.

Remove the red pepper pod, if used, and taste for seasoning – the gumbo should be spicy without destroying the flavors of the shellfish. Serve over boiled rice in bowls.

Gumbo is a corruption of the Bantu word for okra. A Creole dish that is a cross between soup and a stew, it may be made with a variety of ingredients including ham, chicken, shrimps, crabs, oysters and vegetables. However, it is always thickened with the okra from which it takes its name, or with filé powder, ground from sassafras leaves. Both thickeners give the characteristic, slightly sticky consistency to the gumbo.

Saucer Pancakes

$\frac{1}{4}$ cup butter
grated rind of $\frac{1}{2}$ lemon
$\frac{1}{2}$ cup sugar
2 eggs, separated
$\frac{3}{4}$ cup warm milk
$\frac{1}{2}$ cup self-rising flour
pinch of salt
$\frac{1}{2}$ cup apricot or dark cherry jam, melted
extra sugar (for sprinkling)
yogurt sauce (to serve)

Eight 5–5$\frac{1}{2}$ inch ovenproof saucers or foil pie pans

Method

Butter the saucers or pie pans and set oven at moderately hot (375°F).

Cream the butter in a bowl with the lemon rind, gradually add the sugar and beat until light and soft. Stir in the egg yolks and milk.

Sift the flour with the salt; beat the egg whites until they hold a stiff peak. Fold the flour and egg white alternately in 2–3 portions into the butter and sugar mixture, using a metal spoon.

Pour the batter into the prepared saucers or pans until three-quarters full and bake in heated oven for 10–15 minutes or until risen and brown.

Turn out the 'pancakes', sandwich them with melted jam, sprinkle with sugar and serve at once with yogurt sauce.

Upside-down Gingerbread

1 cup flour
$\frac{1}{2}$ teaspoon baking soda
$\frac{1}{4}$ teaspoon salt
2 teaspoons cinnamon
1 teaspoon ground ginger
$\frac{1}{4}$ teaspoon ground nutmeg
$\frac{1}{4}$ teaspoon ground cloves
1 egg, beaten to mix
$\frac{1}{2}$ cup dark brown sugar
6 tablespoons molasses
$\frac{1}{2}$ cup buttermilk
$\frac{1}{4}$ cup shortening, melted

For topping
$\frac{1}{4}$ cup butter
$\frac{1}{2}$ cup dark brown sugar
1 medium can (16 oz) pear halves, drained
6–8 walnut halves
whipped cream, yogurt sauce or cream cheese sauce (to serve) – optional

9 inch springform pan or 8 inch square cake pan

Method

To make the topping: melt the butter, add the sugar and stir for 1–2 minutes over gentle heat to make a smooth syrup; spoon into the pan. Arrange the pears in the pan, cut side down, with walnuts in the gaps.

Set the oven at moderate (350°F).

To make the gingerbread: sift the flour with the baking soda, salt and spices. Mix together the egg, sugar, molasses, buttermilk and cooled shortening. Make a well in the flour, add the molasses mixture and beat hard for 1 minute or until the batter is very smooth. Pour over the topping.

Bake gingerbread in heated oven for 45–50 minutes or until a skewer inserted in center comes out clean.

Turn out the gingerbread onto a platter while still warm and serve. If you like, serve whipped cream, yogurt sauce or cream cheese sauce separately.

Serve upside-down gingerbread with a yogurt sauce or cream cheese sauce, or with whipped cream, if you like

Yogurt Sauce

Whip $\frac{1}{2}$ cup heavy cream until it holds a soft shape. Fold in 1 carton (1 cup) plain yogurt and serve.

Cream Cheese Sauce

Beat $\frac{3}{4}$ cup light cream into 1 small package (3 oz) cream cheese to form a smooth sauce that pours easily. If you like, sweeten with a little sugar.

Arrange the pears, cut side down, and the walnut halves in the pan and cover them with the gingerbread mixture

Chicken Alsacienne, stuffed with pilaf, is served with a rich brown sauce (recipe is on page 72)

STUFFED CHICKEN IS A SPECIAL ENTREE

Leeks Vinaigrette
or
Herring and Apple Salad

Stuffed Chicken Alsacienne
or
Tournedos à la Russe
Green Beans   Parisienne Potatoes

Soufflé Monte Cristo

White wine (with Chicken) – Riesling (Alsace) or Traminer (California)

Red wine (with Tournedos) – Pauillac (Médoc) or Cabernet Sauvignon (California)

With the chicken Alsacienne stuffed with rice and served in a rich brown sauce, no wine will do as well as one from Alsace. Alsatian wines are almost entirely white and are sold by grape name – a system already familiar to many Americans. For a U.S. equivalent, try a California Traminer; it has much the same light, yet spicy quality as the wines of Alsace.

If you choose the tournedos, you'll want a red wine and it should be a fine one to match the splendid simplicity of this cut of beef. Certainly the most distinguished red wine town of Bordeaux's Médoc district is Pauillac, with more top châteaux vineyards – including Lafite, Latour and Mouton-Rothschild – than any other. Virtually any Pauillac wine from a good year – preferably about 7 years old – will be a rare treat. For an American counterpart, try a Cabernet Sauvignon from a top San Francisco Bay area producer.

TIMETABLE

Day before
Make the dressing for the leeks but do not add the currants or sugar.
Pit olives for the steaks.
Make chocolate caraque and store in airtight container in a cool place.
Make espagnole sauce for chicken.

Morning
Prepare and cook the leeks *or prepare herring* but do not arrange in a serving dish. Soak the currants.
Make the soufflé and refrigerate. Soak the macaroons.
Prepare the chicken for roasting and make the stock; make the pilaf.
Marinate the steaks. Prepare Parisienne potatoes and keep in cold water.
Prepare the green beans.

Assemble equipment for final cooking from 6:15 for dinner around 8 p.m.

You will find that **cooking times** given in the individual recipes for these dishes have sometimes been adapted in the timetable to help you when cooking and serving this menu as a party meal.

Order of Work

6:15
Set oven at hot (400°F).

6:30
Put chicken in oven to roast. Complete appetizer, cover and chill.
Put macaroons in center of soufflé and decorate.

7:00
Baste chicken and turn.

7:30
Baste chicken and turn. Put pilaf in oven to reheat.
Cook green beans.
Make mushroom garnish for steaks; fry croûtes.
Cook Parisienne potatoes. Keep all warm.

7:45
Carve chicken, fill with rice and arrange on platter; turn oven to low and keep warm. Finish sauce, reheat and spoon a little over chicken.
Heat rolls in oven to serve with leeks.
Drain the beans and refresh.
Cook steaks, arrange on a platter with the garnish and keep warm.

8:00
Serve appetizer.
Reheat green beans in butter just before serving.

Appetizer

Leeks Vinaigrette

8–12 medium leeks
$\frac{1}{3}$ cup currants, soaked in boiling water for 1 hour
1 tomato, peeled, chopped and sieved, or 1 tablespoon tomato paste mixed with 1 tablespoon water
2 tablespoons red wine vinegar
4–5 tablespoons oil
salt and pepper
1 teaspoon sugar (or to taste)

Method
Trim most of the green from the leeks, wash leeks thoroughly under running water, pulling apart the largest to wash out the grit. Cook in boiling salted water for 5–8 minutes or until tender. Drain the leeks, refresh and drain again. Drain and dry the currants.

Put the sieved tomato or diluted tomato paste into a bowl with the vinegar, oil and seasoning. Mix together and sweeten to taste with a little sugar; add the currants.

Split the leeks lengthwise and arrange them in a dish. Spoon the dressing over and chill slightly. Serve with hot fresh rolls and butter.

Alternative appetizer

Herring and Apple Salad

2 jars (8 oz each) herring fillets in wine sauce
2 crisp dessert apples
1–2 tablespoons lemon juice
salt and pepper
$\frac{1}{4}$ cup rice
2–3 tablespoons oil
1 tablespoon white wine vinegar
1 teaspoon prepared mustard
a few lettuce leaves (to serve) – optional

Method
Drain the herring fillets, sprinkle them generously with lemon juice and season. Let stand for at least 1 hour.

Boil the rice in plenty of salted water for 12 minutes or until tender, drain and spread it out on a plate to dry.

A short time before serving, mix the oil and vinegar together, season well, add the mustard and mix the dressing with the herring fillets.

Pare, core and slice the apples and add to the herring with the rice. Serve in a bowl or on individual plates garnished with lettuce leaves.

For an appetizer, serve leeks vinaigrette with hot rolls and butter

A special entrée

Split the cooked leeks lengthwise before arranging in a dish and coating with dressing

Entrée

Stuffed Chicken Alsacienne

3$\frac{1}{2}$–4 lb roasting chicken
3 tablespoons butter
salt and pepper
$\frac{1}{2}$ cup sherry
1$\frac{1}{2}$ cups stock (made from chicken giblets, except liver, with root vegetables and seasoning)

For pilaf
1 cup rice
$\frac{1}{2}$ lb piece of bacon
bouquet garni
2 tablespoons butter
1 medium onion, finely chopped
2–2$\frac{1}{2}$ cups chicken stock
$\frac{1}{2}$ bay leaf

For espagnole sauce
3 tablespoons oil
2 tablespoons finely diced onion
2 tablespoons finely diced carrot
1 tablespoon finely diced celery
1$\frac{1}{2}$ tablespoons flour
$\frac{1}{2}$ teaspoon tomato paste
1 tablespoon chopped mushrooms
2$\frac{1}{2}$ cups well-flavored brown stock
bouquet garni

Method

Cook the bacon for the pilaf with the bouquet garni and enough water to cover for 1 hour. Cool in the liquid, then discard bouquet garni and water and chop the bacon finely or grind it.

Set oven at hot (400°F).

Rub the skin of the chicken with 2 tablespoons of the butter, season the inside with salt and pepper and put in remaining butter. Place the bird in a roasting pan with $\frac{1}{4}$ cup sherry and $\frac{3}{4}$ cup stock and roast in heated oven for 1$\frac{1}{4}$–1$\frac{1}{2}$ hours or until no pink juice runs out when the thickest part of the thigh is pierced with a skewer. Baste and turn the chicken from one side to the other and finally onto its back during cooking.

To prepare the pilaf: melt the butter in a flameproof casserole, fry the onion until soft, add the rice and cook slowly for a few minutes until the rice is transparent. Add 2 cups stock and bring to a boil. With a fork stir in the finely chopped bacon. Add the bay leaf, cover the casserole tightly and cook in the oven with the chicken for 15 minutes. Add more stock if the pot is dry and cook 5–7 minutes longer or until the rice is tender. Remove bay leaf.

Make the espagnole sauce (see Volume 2).

Transfer the chicken to a carving board, carve suprêmes from the side of the breast and cut away the breastbone with scissors. Put the chicken on a platter, fill the body cavity with the pilaf, slice the suprêmes and replace them on the bird. Use just enough pilaf to fill the cavity of the chicken and serve the rest separately.

Discard any fat from the roasting pan and dissolve the pan sediment with remaining $\frac{3}{4}$ cup stock and $\frac{1}{4}$ cup sherry; strain into the espagnole sauce. Simmer it until well reduced and the flavor is concentrated.

Spoon a little of the sauce over the chicken and serve the rest separately. Serve with buttered green beans.

Remove the suprêmes from each side of the chicken; then with scissors, cut away the breastbone of the chicken ready for filling the body cavity with pilaf

After the body cavity has been well filled with some of the pilaf, replace the sliced suprêmes on top before spooning the sauce over the chicken

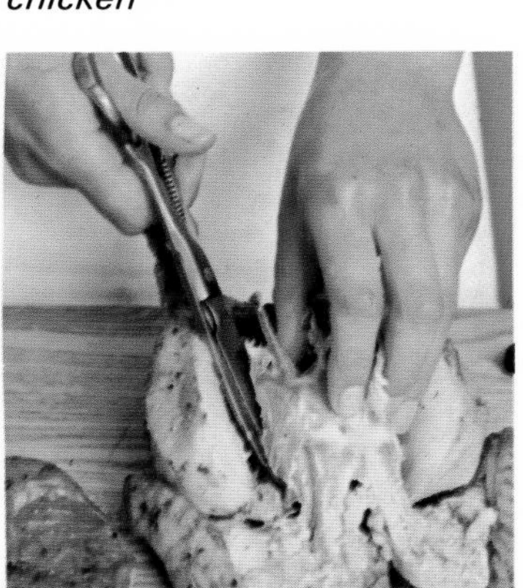

A suprême is all the white meat on the breast down to the wing bone on a chicken. It should be removed in one piece from the bones on each side.

Alternative entrée

Tournedos à la Russe

4 tournedos steaks or fillet steaks
1–2 tablespoons brandy or sherry
black pepper, freshly ground
4–5 tablespoons clarified butter (for frying)
4 croûtes, cut to fit steaks

For garnish
2 cups ($\frac{1}{2}$ lb) mushrooms
3 tablespoons butter
salt and pepper
$\frac{1}{2}$ cup red or white wine or well-flavored stock
6–8 green olives, pitted and reshaped
juice of $\frac{1}{2}$ lemon
$\frac{1}{4}$ cup sour cream

Tournedos are round steaks cut 1$\frac{1}{2}$–2 inches thick from a fillet of beef. Fillet steaks are like tournedos except the 'tail' is not trimmed.

Method

Lay the steaks on a dish, sprinkle with brandy or sherry and freshly ground black pepper. Let stand for about 1 hour.

To make the garnish: cut the mushroom stalks level with the caps (this helps them keep their shape) and wipe the caps with a damp cloth, if necessary. Sauté them quickly for 1 minute in the butter, season, add the wine or stock and cook until the liquid is reduced a little. Remove pan from the heat.

Heat some of the clarified butter in a frying pan or skillet and fry the croûtes until golden brown. Remove them

The alternative entrée, tournedos à la Russe, has an olive and mushroom garnish, with green beans and Parisienne potatoes for accompaniments

from the pan. Drain the steaks, reserving the marinade.

Add a little more clarified butter to the pan, put in the steaks and fry briskly for 3–3$\frac{1}{2}$ minutes on each side (for rare steak).

While the steaks are frying, add the olives, lemon juice and sour cream to the mushrooms and shake the pan to mix them (stirring might break the olives and mushrooms). Add any marinade left from the steaks and heat well without boiling.

Serve the steaks on the croûtes, and spoon the mushroom and olive garnish down one side of the platter. Serve with buttered green beans, and parisienne potatoes.

To Pit and Reshape Olives

Make a small cut across the top of the olive (but not completely through it) with a small sharp knife. Then, keeping the blade of knife against the pit, work in a spiral removing the flesh as you go until you get to the base of the pit; remove the flesh from the bottom. Reshape the olive.

Black olives are usually softer than green ones and can be pitted by slitting down one side and using the point of a small knife to lever out pit.

Parisienne Potatoes

5–6 large potatoes, peeled
$\frac{1}{4}$ cup butter
salt

Method

Scoop out balls from the potatoes with a ball cutter.

In a skillet melt the butter and sauté the potatoes over medium heat for 10–15 minutes or until tender, shaking the pan so the balls brown evenly. Sprinkle them with a little salt just before serving.

Spectacular soufflé Monte Cristo is filled with liqueur-soaked macaroons and decorated with rosettes of whipped cream and chocolate caraque

Dessert

Soufflé Monte Cristo

3 eggs, separated
$\frac{1}{4}$ cup sugar
2 cups milk
$\frac{1}{2}$ vanilla bean, split (with $\frac{1}{2}$ teaspoon vanilla extract) – optional or 1 teaspoon vanilla extract
1 envelope gelatin
$\frac{1}{4}$ cup water
1 cup heavy cream, whipped until it holds a soft shape
chocolate caraque, made from 3 squares (3 oz) semisweet chocolate
5 almond macaroons, broken in pieces to make 1$\frac{1}{2}$ cups
2–3 tablespoons brandy, rum or liqueur such as Cointreau or Grand Marnier
$\frac{1}{2}$ cup heavy cream, stiffly whipped (for decoration)

Soufflé dish (1 quart capacity); 8 oz bottle; pastry bag and medium star tube

Method

Tie a strip of lightly oiled wax or silicone paper (oiled side inside) around the soufflé dish to form a collar extending 3 inches above the edge of the dish. Lightly oil the bottle and stand it in the center of the dish.

In a bowl beat the egg yolks with the sugar until the mixture is light and thick. Heat the milk to scalding with vanilla bean, if using. Cover and infuse off the heat for 10 minutes.

Remove the vanilla bean and gradually pour the milk into the yolk mixture. Pour it back into the pan and stir over low heat until the custard thickens enough to coat the back of a spoon. Do not let it boil. Strain and cool. If using vanilla extract, add at this point – a little may also be needed to accent the flavor of the vanilla bean.

In a small pan sprinkle the gelatin over the water and let stand 5 minutes or until spongy. Stand the pan in hot water, heat gently until the gelatin is dissolved and stir into the custard. Stand it on ice or in ice water, stirring often. Beat the egg whites until they hold a stiff peak.

Remove the custard mixture from the ice as soon as it is cold and on the point of setting, and fold in the lightly whipped cream and stiffly beaten egg whites. Pour the soufflé mixture into the dish, layering it with chocolate caraque and reserving some of the caraque for decoration. Chill 2–3 hours or until set.

Watchpoint: several ice cubes in the bottle will speed the setting time.

Put the macaroon pieces in a bowl and sprinkle them generously with the chosen brandy, rum or liqueur.

When ready to serve the soufflé, gently twist the bottle and carefully lift it out. Immediately fill the cavity with macaroons. Trim the paper collar level with the soufflé. Fill the pastry bag fitted with a medium star tube with the stiffly whipped cream, pipe the rosettes around the edge of the soufflé and decorate with remaining chocolate caraque. Peel off the paper collar just before serving.

For soufflé Monte Cristo: layer the thickened soufflé mixture with most of the chocolate caraque in the prepared soufflé dish. Chill the soufflé until set before removing the bottle and filling the cavity with macaroons

Chocolate Caraque

Melt 3 squares (3 oz) semisweet chocolate, grated or chopped, on a heatproof plate over a pan of hot water. Work with a metal spatula until the chocolate is smooth and spread it thinly on a marble slab or Formica-type surface. Leave until it is nearly set.

Hold a sharp, long knife almost at a right angle to the chocolate surface; shave off long chocolate scrolls or flakes using a slight sideways sawing movement.

Caraque looks better when fresh but can be kept a day or two in an airtight container.

For chocolate caraque, hold a sharp knife or spatula at a right angle to the chocolate and shave off long scrolls

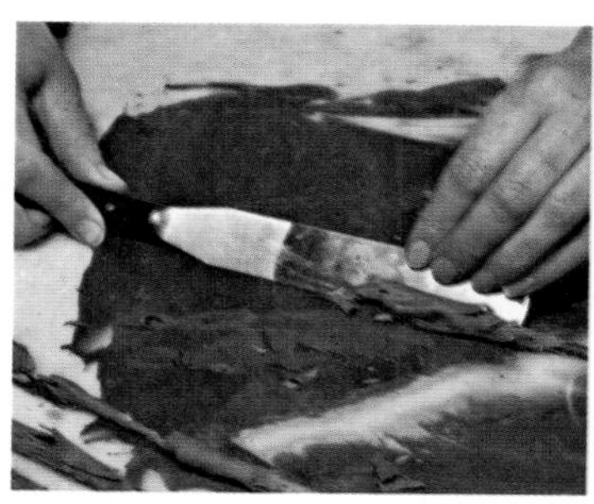

VIN
BLAN
EAU

COOKING WITH WINE

Wine is an indispensable ingredient in innumerable gourmet dishes and many combinations like coq au vin or scaloppine with marsala are renowned.

Certain wines go best with certain foods – for cooking as well as for drinking and as a general rule, you won't go wrong if you cook a dish with the same type of wine you would drink with it. The chart on page 78 gives detailed suggestions on how to match dishes with their complementary wines.

The better the wine you add to a dish, the better it will taste, but you can reserve expensive vintage wines for cooking for special occasions as a modest wine is quite adequate for most dishes. Avoid inferior wines or liquors in cooking as their harsh flavor will always overwhelm all other ingredients.

If you use wine only for cooking, try to buy half instead of whole bottles, as wine turns vinegary after it has been opened for a week or two. To discourage this, decant leftover wine into a small bottle so there is very little air between the wine and cork, then cork the bottle tightly.

There is no really satisfactory substitute for wine in cooking, so if you prefer not to use it, look for recipes that do not call for it.

USES OF WINE IN COOKING

The table below is a guide to choosing the **right wine for cooking.** The white wines are listed according to their degree of sweetness, starting with the dry ones. The red wines are listed according to their relative fullness, starting with the light ones. Rosé wines are not generally used for cooking. Variations in vinification and vintage make these rankings approximate, and the suggestions for both wines and compatible foods are not intended to be exclusive.

WHITE WINES

Foreign	Domestic	For use with
Burgundy (Chablis)	Chardonnay	Oysters; clams
Bordeaux (Graves)	Dry Sémillon; Diamond	Scallops; shrimps
Burgundy (Côte de Beaune)	Pinot Chardonnay	Flounder; halibut; chicken; veal
Burgundy (Mâconnais)	Pinot Blanc	Pâté; sweetbreads; chicken; veal
Loire (Pouilly)	Dry Sauvignon Blanc; Delaware	Trout; salmon; chicken; veal
Loire (Vouvray)	Chenin Blanc; Delaware	Crab; lobster; brains
Rhine (Mosel, Rheingau)	Johannisberg Riesling; Niagara or Elvira	Turkey; pork; fresh fruits
Rhine (Hessia, Pfalz)	Sylvaner; Niagara or Elvira	Turkey; ham; fresh fruits
Alsace (Gewürztraminer)	Gewürztraminer	Light desserts
Bordeaux (Sauternes)	Sweet Sauvignon Blanc; Catawba or Sweet Sémillon	Rich desserts

RED WINES

Foreign	Domestic	For use with
Burgundy (Beaujolais)	Gamay Beaujolais	Pâté; chicken; veal
Bordeaux (Médoc, Pomerol)	Cabernet Sauvignon; Chelois	Lamb; chicken; veal; cheese
Burgundy (Côte de Nuits, Côte de Beaune)	Pinot Noir; Baco Noir	Roast beef; steak; cheese
Rhône (Châteauneuf du Pape, Hermitage)	Zinfandel; Petit Syrah	Game; kidneys; cheese

FORTIFIED WINE

In addition to the natural wines listed left, there are several 'fortified wines' – natural wines to which brandy has been added – that have wide application in flavoring meats, sauces, desserts, etc. In most cases, the foreign and domestic versions bear the same names. The higher alcohol content of these wines gives a more pronounced flavor and the quantities required are usually about half that of natural wines. The additional alcohol also makes them useful in flaming dishes. The principal fortified wines and some of their uses are listed below.

Madeira

Sweet, brown wine (from the island of the same name) whose rich, dark flavors are a boon to braised meats, game sauces, etc.

Marsala

Another sweet, strong wine with a uniquely attractive bouquet and taste that lends itself to such varied dishes as escalopes de veau and zabaione.

Port

Sweet, red wine that is widely served with or after a dessert, but which also may be added to game sauces and served over fresh fruit.

Sherry

Perhaps the most universally known fortified wine and one that varies enormously in its characteristics; the richer, sweeter varieties are ideal for cooking with kidneys and dark meats, for adding to sauces and soups and for flavoring desserts like wine gelatins.

Vermouth

White or red fortified wine to which various herb essences have been added; an extremely useful flavoring for chicken, veal and fish, so long as its characteristics do not conflict with or overly reinforce the spices called for in the recipe.

To Prepare Wine for Cooking

Both red and white wines should be reduced to evaporate the alcohol and leave the mellow essence of the wine. When wine is added at the beginning of a dish – such as a braise or pot roast – reduction is done during the long cooking. If wine is added toward end of cooking, reduce it first in a separate pan by bringing to a boil and boiling rapidly. If done in a shallow pan over a flame, the alcohol in the wine may catch fire – let it burn out and continue reduction as usual.

Red wine is usually reduced by about one-eighth and white wine even more so – the amount will be given in specific recipes. An exception is white wine added to a court bouillon for fish – here the alcohol in the wine adds necessary acidity to the mixture.

Shrimp Kebabs

$1\frac{1}{2}$ lb large uncooked, peeled shrimps
5–6 bay leaves
6 tablespoons melted butter (for brushing)
black pepper, freshly ground
$\frac{1}{2}$ teaspoon paprika
$\frac{1}{4}$ cup fresh white breadcrumbs (optional)
lemon wedges (for serving)

For marinade
1 cup white wine
1 teaspoon tarragon
2 tablespoons oil
$\frac{1}{2}$ teaspoon thyme
1 clove of garlic, crushed (optional)

8 kebab skewers

Method

Combine the ingredients for the marinade, adding garlic if you like, and pour over the shrimps. Mix well, cover and let stand in the refrigerator for 4–5 hours.

Drain the shrimps. Break bay leaves into 2–3 pieces. Thread shrimps on skewers with a piece of bay leaf between every second or third shrimp.

To broil or barbecue: brush kebabs generously with melted butter, sprinkle with black pepper and paprika and broil or grill with the rack about 3 inches from the heat for 2–4 minutes on each side or until shrimps are well browned and just tender. Turn once during cooking and baste often with melted butter.

To bake: set kebabs in a shallow baking dish, spoon over melted butter and sprinkle with black pepper, paprika and $\frac{1}{4}$ cup fresh breadcrumbs, if you like. Bake in a hot oven (400°F) for 10–12 minutes or until the shrimps are browned and just tender. Turn once and baste often with melted butter during cooking.

Serve shrimp kebabs with lemon wedges and savory saffron rice.

Savory Saffron Rice

1 cup rice
pinch of saffron, soaked for 30 minutes in 2 tablespoons boiling water
2 tablespoons butter
4 slices of bacon
1 small onion, thinly sliced
salt and pepper

Method

Cook the rice in plenty of boiling salted water for about 12 minutes or until tender. Drain in a colander, rinse with hot water and let rice stand until thoroughly drained.

Melt the butter in a frying pan, add the bacon slices and fry until brown and crisp. Remove the bacon from the pan and drain on paper towels. When cold, crumble into small pieces.

Add the onion to the pan and cook slowly until golden brown. Stir in the rice and add the saffron liquid. With a fork, toss the rice over heat, adding more butter if necessary to make a rich but fluffy mixture. Season with salt and pepper and stir in the bacon.

Crab Mousse

2 cups (1 lb) cooked crab meat
velouté sauce (made with 2 tablespoons butter, 2 tablespoons flour and $1\frac{1}{2}$ cups fish or chicken stock)
salt and pepper
1 envelope gelatin
$\frac{1}{4}$ cup white wine
$\frac{3}{4}$ cup mayonnaise (see page 21)
$\frac{3}{4}$ cup heavy cream, whipped until it holds a soft shape

For garnish
2 cucumbers, peeled and sliced
$\frac{1}{4}$ cup vinaigrette dressing
$\frac{1}{2}$ teaspoon paprika
dash of Tabasco

Soufflé dish ($1\frac{1}{2}$ quart capacity) or 7 inch springform pan

Method

Lightly oil the soufflé dish or cake pan.

Make velouté sauce, season well and cool.

Sprinkle the gelatin over the wine in a small pan, dissolve over a pan of hot water and stir into the velouté sauce with the mayonnaise.

Separate the crab meat flakes as much as possible and stir into the mixture with a fork. Chill in the refrigerator or over a bowl of ice water, stirring occasionally, until the mixture is on the point of setting. Fold in the whipped cream, taste for seasoning and pour into the prepared dish or pan. Cover and chill at least 2 hours or until set.

To prepare garnish: sprinkle cucumber slices with a little salt and let stand for 30 minutes to draw out the juices (dégorger). Rinse with cold water and drain. Season the vinaigrette dressing with the paprika and a good dash of Tabasco and mix with the cucumber.

A short time before serving, unmold the crab mousse onto a platter and spoon over the cucumber slices.

To unmold a creamy mixture: tilt the mold sideways and break the airlock by inserting the point of a knife between the mixture and the mold. Turn the mold in a circle so the mixture loosens all around. Put a plate upside down on top of the mold, quickly invert the mold and plate, holding them together. Shake gently and the mold will slip out onto the plate.

Kidney Soup

$\frac{1}{2}$ lb lambs' or veal kidneys
5 cups brown stock
bouquet garni
2 tablespoons butter
1 onion, chopped
$1\frac{1}{2}$ tablespoons flour
2 teaspoons tomato paste
salt and pepper
$\frac{1}{2}$ cup red wine or $\frac{1}{4}$ cup sherry
2–3 slices of bread, crusts removed, cut in cubes and fried in 3–4 tablespoons oil and butter, mixed (for croûtons) – optional

For liaison (optional)
1 teaspoon arrowroot (mixed to a paste with 1 tablespoon cold water)

Method

Remove skin from kidneys, if necessary, cut out the cores with scissors and slice the kidneys thinly.

Combine the slices in a kettle with half the stock and bouquet garni, cover, bring to a boil and simmer 1 hour or until kidneys are very tender. Remove bouquet garni and pour the mixture into a bowl.

Melt the butter in kettle and brown the onion. Stir in the flour and tomato paste, add remaining stock with seasoning and stir until boiling. Add the wine or sherry and kidney mixture to the stock, season and simmer 10 minutes.

Fry the croûtons, drain on paper towels and keep warm.

Purée the soup in a blender or work through a food mill or sieve. Reheat and thicken it if necessary, by stirring in the arrowroot paste and cooking until the soup thickens. Serve with croûtons, if you like.

Rognons Sauté au Vin Blanc (Kidneys Sautéed in White Wine)

8–10 lambs' kidneys
$\frac{3}{4}$ cup dry white wine
3–4 tablespoons butter
1 small onion, chopped
1 cup ($\frac{1}{4}$ lb) mushrooms, sliced
1 tablespoon flour
$\frac{1}{2}$ cup stock
salt and pepper
2–3 tablespoons heavy cream

Method

Remove the skin from the kidneys, if necessary, cut in half and cut out the cores with scissors. Boil the wine until reduced by one-third.

In a skillet or a shallow flameproof casserole, heat 2 tablespoons butter and, when foaming, add kidneys, cut side down. Sauté for 2–3 minutes, take out and keep warm.

Lower the heat, add the onion and mushrooms and, when they are soft, add the remaining butter and stir in the flour. Cook gently for 1 minute, add the wine and stock and stir until boiling.

Replace the kidneys (discard any juice as this spoils the appearance and flavor of the sauce), season and simmer 12–15 minutes. Stir in the cream, bring just back to a boil and transfer to a warm platter. Serve with boiled potatoes and green beans.

Sauté of Liver Italienne

8 slices of calf's liver or 2 cups (1 lb) chicken livers
6 tablespoons butter
1 medium onion, finely chopped
1 cup ($\frac{1}{4}$ lb) mushrooms, finely chopped
$\frac{1}{4}$ cup white wine
$1\frac{1}{2}$ teaspoons tomato paste
$\frac{1}{2}$ cup stock
$\frac{1}{2}$ cup ($\frac{1}{4}$ lb) cooked ham, diced
2 tablespoons flour
pinch of ground mace or nutmeg
salt and pepper
1 tablespoon chopped parsley
1 teaspoon mixed herbs (chervil, tarragon)

Method

In a saucepan heat 3 tablespoons butter, add the onion and cook gently until soft. Add mushrooms, increase the heat and cook quickly for 3–4 minutes until all the liquid has evaporated. Add the wine and boil to reduce a little. Stir in the tomato paste and stock, cover and cook gently for 10 minutes. Add the ham and warm over low heat.

Sift the flour with the mace or nutmeg and season to taste; coat the liver with the seasoned flour.

Melt remaining butter in a skillet and sauté the liver quickly for 3 minutes on each side or until lightly browned, shaking the pan frequently to prevent it from sticking.

Arrange the liver on a warm platter, add the herbs to the mushroom mixture, taste for seasoning and spoon over the liver.

Lamb Banyuls

3–$3\frac{1}{2}$ lb loin of lamb
2 tablespoons butter

For sauce and garnish
3–4 (1 lb) large onions, very thinly sliced
3–4 tablespoons butter
1 cup red Burgundy
salt and pepper
$1\frac{1}{2}$ cups well-flavored stock
$\frac{3}{4}$ cup heavy cream
2 teaspoons arrowroot

Method

Score the fat of the meat in a wide lattice pattern and spread it with butter. Roast in a moderately hot oven (375°F), allowing 18 minutes per lb and 18 minutes more for medium cooked lamb. Baste often during roasting.

To prepare the sauce and garnish: sauté the onion slices slowly in butter, stirring occasionally until golden brown. Add half the wine, season and cook 5–10 minutes. Drain the onions, reserving the liquid, and arrange them down the center of a warm platter.

Take the lamb from the pan and keep warm. Discard fat from the pan, leaving the sediment. Add half the stock and bring to a boil, stirring, to dissolve the pan juices. Strain into a pan, add the remaining wine, bring to a boil and reduce for 1–2 minutes. Add reserved liquid from onions, taste for seasoning and add the cream. Mix the arrowroot with remaining stock, stir into the sauce and bring just to a boil, stirring until it thickens.

Carve the lamb into chops, arrange them, bones pointing up, on the onions and spoon over a little of the sauce. Serve the remaining sauce separately with château potatoes and a green vegetable such as broccoli.

Ragoût of beef Bourguignon is garnished with fried croûtes

Ragoût of Beef Bourguignon

$1\frac{1}{2}$–2 lb chuck or round steak, cut into 2 inch squares
$\frac{1}{4}$ lb piece of bacon
10–12 small onions, peeled
1 cup red Burgundy
2–3 tablespoons oil
1 tablespoon flour
$1\frac{1}{2}$–2 cups stock
1 clove of garlic, crushed
1 teaspoon tomato paste
bouquet garni
salt and pepper
2 cups ($\frac{1}{2}$ lb) mushrooms
1 tablespoon chopped parsley
2–3 slices of bread, crusts removed, cut in triangles and fried in 3–4 tablespoons oil and butter, mixed (for croûtes)

Method

Cut the bacon into thick strips and blanch with the onions by putting into cold water, bringing to a boil and cooking for 2 minutes. Drain them.

Boil the wine until it is reduced by about one-eighth.

In a flameproof casserole heat the oil and brown the meat on all sides, a few pieces at a time. Take them out and keep warm. Add blanched onions and the bacon and cook slowly until browned.

Watchpoint: remove the onions from the casserole after browning and replace them in the ragoût after the first hour of cooking, otherwise they tend to become mushy and spoil the appearance of the dish.

Stir the flour into the pan and cook until lightly browned. Pour in the wine and $1\frac{1}{2}$ cups stock, stir in garlic, tomato paste and bouquet garni and put back the meat.

Bring the mixture slowly to a boil, shaking the pan gently – add more stock if needed to cover the meat. Season lightly, cover the pan and simmer gently on top of the stove or in a moderately low oven (325°F) for $1\frac{1}{2}$–2 hours or until the meat is very tender. After 1 hour replace the onions.

About 15 minutes before the end of cooking, add mushrooms, trimming the stems level with the caps. Fry the croûtes until golden brown on both sides and drain on paper towels.

Remove the bouquet garni, taste ragoût for seasoning, and transfer to a warm serving dish, if you like, or serve in the casserole. Sprinkle with chopped parsley and arrange the croûtes around the dish.

A ragoût is made of pieces of meat, poultry or fish that are slowly stewed with liquid, often with vegetables added. Sometimes the ingredients are browned in oil before cooking, as for ragoût of beef bourguignon; sometimes they are cooked without browning as for Irish stew.

Cold Burgundian Ham with Parsley

$1\frac{1}{2}$ lb cooked ham, thickly sliced

For wine gelatin
5 cups well-flavored chicken or veal stock
1–2 envelopes gelatin (optional)
$\frac{3}{4}$ cup white Burgundy (for example, Mâcon)
2 teaspoons tarragon or white wine vinegar
2 egg whites
$\frac{1}{4}$ cup chopped parsley

Glass bowl ($2\frac{1}{2}$ quart capacity)

Homemade jellied stock is essential for this dish of ham set in a white wine gelatin. It is traditionally served on Easter Sunday in the Burgundy region of France.

Method

To make wine gelatin: chill the stock until it is firmly set, then skim off any fat. If not firmly set, add 1–2 envelopes gelatin; sprinkle the gelatin over $\frac{1}{2}$ cup stock and let stand 5 minutes until spongy; reserve. Put the stock in a large kettle with the wine and vinegar, melt over gentle heat and taste for seasoning – it should be highly seasoned.

Whisk egg whites until frothy, add to the pan with the gelatin, if used, and bring to a boil over medium heat, whisking with a backwards and downwards motion so the egg whites are thoroughly mixed into the wine and stock.

As soon as the mixture boils, stop whisking so the egg whites can form a crust on the surface and let this crust boil to the top of the pan. Take from the heat and leave 5 minutes until the contents subside. Bring to a boil to the top of the pan twice more without whisking, then cool 10 minutes.

Lay a scalded dish towel or cloth over a bowl and carefully ladle all the gelatin mixture into it. Lift up the cloth, tie the ends with string and hang it from a hook or door handle so the gelatin can slowly drain through the cloth. The gelatin should be clear and sparkling. Leave until cool but not set.

Cut the ham into 2 inch strips and put a layer at the bottom of the glass bowl. Press down lightly and continue until all the ham is used – the bowl should be half full. Pour over enough cool gelatin to moisten and just cover the ham and chill until set.

Watchpoint: cooked ham soon loses its attractive pink color if left exposed to the air, so keep ham strips covered tightly until gelatin is poured over them.

Add the parsley to remaining gelatin, set it over a bowl of ice water and stir until it is on the point of setting. Pour carefully on top of the ham gelatin, cover and chill 2–3 hours until firmly set. Let gelatin come to room temperature before serving.

Veal Escalopes Coupole

4–8 veal escalopes (about 1 $\frac{1}{2}$ lb)
16–18 small onions
3–4 tablespoons butter
1 cup ($\frac{1}{4}$ lb) mushrooms
$\frac{1}{3}$ cup port
$\frac{3}{4}$ cup well-flavored stock
bouquet garni
salt and pepper
kneaded butter, made with
2 tablespoons butter and
1 tablespoon flour
$\frac{3}{4}$ cup heavy cream

Veal chops can be substituted for the escalopes in this recipe but allow 15–20 minutes cooking time instead of 7–10.

Method

Blanch the onions by putting in cold water, bringing to a boil and boiling 4–5 minutes. Drain and peel them.

In a skillet melt the butter and brown escalopes on both sides over medium heat. Take them out, add the onions and brown. Remove the onions, add mushrooms and cook until soft. Remove the mushrooms and replace the escalopes and onions.

Add the port, heat until almost boiling and flame. Simmer to dissolve the pan juices. When the port is reduced by half, replace the mushrooms and add the stock with bouquet garni and seasoning. Cover pan and simmer gently 7–10 minutes.

Arrange the escalopes and vegetables on a warm platter and keep warm.

Remove bouquet garni, bring gravy to a boil and stir in kneaded butter, a few pieces at a time, until the sauce is the consistency of heavy cream. Simmer 2 minutes, add the cream, simmer 1 minute longer, taste for seasoning and spoon over the veal.

Serve veal escalopes with sautéed potatoes and buttered baby carrots.

To Flamber Dishes

Dishes are flamed (flambéd) with a liquor like brandy or a fortified wine like sherry.

Heat the liquor or wine until it is almost boiling so it catches fire easily, then pour it, flaming, over the dish. The food must be hot and sizzling otherwise the flame will go out. Alternatively the liquor may be heated with the food, then flamed.

Flaming should slightly singe the surface of food; the alcohol is burned out of the liquor so the juices that remain give color and flavor to the food and sauce. Flaming also burns up excess fat.

Dinde Braisé au Champagne
(Turkey Braised with Champagne)

5–6 lb turkey
2 teaspoons arrowroot, mixed to a paste with 2 tablespoons water
potato croquettes (for serving) – see opposite page
morels or mushrooms in cream (for serving) – see right

For braising
1 calf's foot split
2 tablespoons oil
2 tablespoons butter
1 bottle of Champagne
2 onions, sliced
2 carrots, sliced
2 cups beef stock
bouquet garni
salt and papper

Trussing needle and string

Serves 6.

Method

Wash the calf's foot thoroughly and blanch it in boiling water for 5 minutes; drain it. Sprinkle the inside of the turkey with seasoning and truss

In a large flameproof casserole heat the oil and butter and brown the turkey on all sides. Take it out, add the vegetables, cover and cook over low heat for 5–7 minutes or until the fat is absorbed.

Replace the turkey, add the calf's foot, 1 cup stock, about three-quarters of the Champagne, bouquet garni and seasoning. Cover and braise in a moderately low oven (325°F) for 2–2$\frac{1}{2}$ hours or until the turkey is tender and no pink juice runs out when the thigh is pierced with a skewer. Add the remaining Champagne and stock during cooking when the liquid evaporates.

Transfer the turkey to a platter and keep warm. Discard the calf's foot and strain the cooking liquid, pressing well to extract all the juice from the vegetables.

Skim off the fat and boil the liquid to reduce to 2 cups. Stir in the arrowroot paste and bring the sauce just back to a boil, stirring until it thickens. Taste for seasoning, spoon a little sauce over the turkey and serve the rest separately.

Garnish the platter with potato croquettes and serve morels or mushrooms in cream separately.

Morilles à la Crème (Morels with Cream)

1 $\frac{1}{2}$ cups dried or 2 cans (12 oz each) morel mushrooms
1 $\frac{1}{2}$ cups heavy cream
2 tablespoons butter
1 tablespoon flour
salt and pepper
$\frac{1}{4}$ teaspoon nutmeg
$\frac{1}{2}$ cup sour cream

Morels are dark wrinkled mushrooms with a rich aromatic flavor. They grow wild in many areas of the U.S.A. but are very hard to find, so they are expensive. They are available dried or in cans. Serves 6 as an appetizer on toast or in a pastry shell. Serves 6–8 as an accompaniment to an entrée.

Method

Soak dried morels in warm water to cover for 30 minutes and drain, or drain canned morels. Dry them on paper towels.

Heat the butter, add the morels and sauté 2 minutes. Stir in the flour, add the heavy cream and bring to a boil, stirring. Season with salt, pepper and nutmeg and simmer 2 minutes or until the sauce is fairly thick.

Just before serving, stir in the sour cream and reheat without boiling.

Potato Croquettes

Cook 5 medium potatoes in boiling salted water for 15 minutes or until tender. Drain. Work through a strainer or ricer. Return to pan, beat in 2 tablespoons butter, 2 egg yolks, $\frac{1}{4}$ cup of hot milk, salt and pepper.

Cool the potato mixture, roll out onto a floured board into a 1 inch thick cylinder. Cut into 2 inch lengths. Roll the croquettes in flour, seasoned with salt and pepper, and brush them with 1 egg, beaten to mix with $\frac{1}{2}$ teaspoon salt.

Coat the potato croquettes with dry white breadcrumbs. Fry them in butter, turning so they brown evenly, or fry them in hot deep fat (375°F on a fat thermometer) until golden brown. Drain well on paper towels. Serves 6.

Brown the chickens on all sides, then add wine and peeled lemon rind and juice to the pot

Chicken with Lemon

2 broiling chickens (2–2$\frac{1}{2}$ lb each)
2 tablespoons butter
2 shallots, finely chopped
1 cup medium-sweet white wine (like a Rhine or Sylvaner, but not Sauternes)
peeled rind and juice of 1 lemon
1 teaspoon arrowroot (mixed to a paste with 1 tablespoon cold water)
$\frac{1}{4}$ cup heavy cream
1 tablespoon chopped mixed herbs (parsley, tarragon, thyme, rosemary)
salt and pepper
slices of lemon (for garnish)

Method

In a flameproof casserole melt the butter and brown the chickens on all sides. Take them out, add the shallot and cook 1–2 minutes until soft. Replace the chickens, add the wine and lemon rind and juice; cover pan and simmer 25–35 minutes over low heat or until the chickens are very tender. Take them out and keep warm.

If necessary boil the liquid in the pan to reduce to about 1 cup. Discard any fat and stir in the arrowroot paste. Cook, stirring, until the sauce thickens, and add the cream and herbs. Bring just to a boil, taste for seasoning and keep warm.

Split the chickens in half with poultry shears, discarding the backbone, and arrange them, overlapping, on a warm platter. Spoon over the sauce and surround with slices of lemon. Serve with baby carrots, tossed in butter and chopped parsley.

Serve zabaione with cookies or as a sauce for cakes and fruit compôte

Zabaione

For each person allow:
1 egg yolk
1 tablespoon sugar
1 tablespoon Marsala or sweet golden sherry

This popular Italian dessert (sometimes spelled zabaglione or sabayon in French) can be served as a sauce for cakes and fruit compote as well as on its own in a stemmed glass. It is quick to make but does not keep well and should be served within 15 minutes.

Method

Put the egg yolk, sugar and Marsala or sherry into a bowl; place over a pan of hot but not boiling water and whisk steadily until the mixture is very light and almost thick enough to leave a ribbon trail when the whisk is lifted.

Take from heat and continue whisking 1 minute, then pour into warm stemmed glasses. Serve at once with Champagne cookies or amaretti (Italian almond cookies – see page 92).

If you have a copper bowl, use this and a balloon whisk for making zabaione to give a smoother texture and greater volume. Take it to the table and ladle the mixture straight from the bowl into glasses.

Lemon Syllabub

1 lemon
$\frac{1}{2}$ cup Madeira or sweet sherry
$\frac{1}{2}$ cup Sauternes or sweet white wine
4–6 tablespoons sugar
2 cups heavy cream
1 egg white

Method

Thinly peel the rind from the lemon and soak overnight in Madeira or sherry and wine.

Squeeze the juice from the lemon and add to the sugar with the wines, discarding the lemon rind and stir until the sugar has dissolved.

Whip the cream until it holds a soft shape, then gradually add the wine mixture, whisking until the cream again holds a soft shape. Stiffly whip the egg white, fold into the cream and pile the syllabub in stemmed glasses. Chill well and serve with cigarettes Russes or rolled cookies.

Raspberry or Strawberry Syllabub

1 cup raspberry or strawberry juice
1 cup white wine
peeled rind of 1 lemon
3 tablespoons sugar
pinch of ground nutmeg
1 cup heavy cream

The juice of any tart fruit can be used in this recipe.

Method

Put the fruit juice, wine and lemon rind in a bowl, cover and let stand for several hours in the refrigerator or overnight.

Remove the rind and add the sugar, stirring until dissolved. Add the nutmeg and gradually pour in the cream, stirring constantly until the mixture holds a soft peak.

Pour syllabub into a bowl and serve chilled with cigarettes Russes or rolled cookies.

Clafoutis Limousin
(Cherry Pudding from Limoges)

1 lb tart cooking cherries
$\frac{1}{4}$ cup brandy
$\frac{1}{2}$ cup flour
pinch of salt
$\frac{1}{2}$ cup sugar
3 eggs, beaten to mix
1 cup milk
confectioners' sugar (for sprinkling)

Shallow flameproof baking dish ($1\frac{1}{2}$ quart capacity)

Clafoutis is usually made with tart cherries. However, sweet cherries can be used if you halve the quantity of sugar; or cooked pitted prunes, pared, sliced tart apples, or sliced pitted fresh peaches can be substituted for the cherries. There should be about 2 cups prepared fruit – and the amount of sugar needed varies with the tartness of the fruit.

Method

Pit the cherries, add brandy, cover and let stand to macerate for 2–3 hours.

Sift the flour with the salt, add half the sugar and make a well in the center. Add the eggs, stir with the flour until smooth, then gradually stir in the milk and strained juice from cherries.

Thickly butter the dish, pour in half the batter and cook over low heat on top of the stove for about 8–9 minutes or until it begins to set.

Add the remaining sugar to the cherries, spread them on the cooked batter and pour over remaining batter. Bake in a moderate oven (350°F) for 50–55 minutes or until the clafoutis is puffy and golden brown. Cool a little (the clafoutis will begin to sink slightly), sprinkle generously with confectioners' sugar and serve warm, with a bowl of whipped cream if you like.

Make a spectacular chestnut dessert such as Chamonix, or Mont Blanc (at front), based on meringue, and boîte au chocolat (right)

COOKING WITH NUTS

Nuts are valued in cooking for much more than just their high nutrient content. In savory dishes they make unusual combinations of flavor and texture and nuts have always been a favorite ingredient in desserts, cakes and cookies.

Chestnut purée gives a superb smoothness to cream and chocolate mixtures; walnuts have a delicious crunchy texture; almonds lend a delicate fragrance to the flavor of any dish and their high proportion of oil adds richness. Pecans, too, add richness to cakes and cookies, and pistachios have a flavor all their own. The inventory of nut recipes is endless – here are just a few ideas.

Preparation of Nuts

Blanched Nuts
Cover nuts with boiling water and let them stand 5 minutes. Drain and, when cool enough to handle, slip off the skins.

Ground or Grated Nuts
If possible, use a special nut mill or rotary cheese grater or work a few nuts at a time in a blender.

Shredded Nuts
After blanching and skinning, cut horizontally into flakes with a sharp knife.

Slivered Nuts
After blanching and skinning, split in two, cut each half lengthwise in sticks.

Salted Nuts
Heat about 2 tablespoons salad oil for each cup of nuts. Stir in the nuts and cook over moderate heat, stirring constantly, until they are golden brown. Remove with a slotted spoon and drain on paper towels. While still hot, sprinkle the nuts with salt, preferably coarse salt.

Roasted (Browned) Nuts
Scatter nuts on a baking sheet and bake them in a moderate oven (350°F) until golden brown, turning occasionally.

Toasted Nuts
Sprinkle nuts on a baking sheet and broil them about 5–6 inches from the broiling unit. Watch them closely and turn frequently until golden brown.

Deep Fat Fried Nuts
Heat oil in a deep fat fryer to 360°F on a fat thermometer. In a fine wire basket add nuts and fry a handful at a time for several minutes until they are golden brown. Drain nuts on paper towels and sprinkle with salt.

To Freeze Nuts
Put nut kernels in a freezer container or in a plastic bag. Squeeze out all air possible before tying securely. (You can refreeze them after thawing.)

Nut Milk
To make ½ cup nut milk: infuse 2 tablespoons ground almonds or dried coconut in ¾ cup boiling water for 1 hour – squeeze the mixture in cheesecloth to extract the milk. This liquid is used for making curry dishes.

To Skin Chestnuts
Pierce each nut with a pointed knife. In a saucepan cover the chestnuts with cold water, bring to a boil and take from the heat. Lift nuts from the water with a slotted spoon, a few at a time, hold them with a cloth and strip away the shell and inner skin with a small sharp knife. If skin does not peel easily, put nut back in hot water for another minute.

If the water cools, bring it just back to a boil; do not let water boil for more than ½ minute or nuts will overcook and peel and skin will be impossible to remove.

One pound of chestnuts in the shell yields about 2½ cups shelled chestnuts.

To Cook Skinned Chestnuts
Put them in a pan and cover with a mixture of half milk, half water. Cover and simmer gently for 20–30 minutes or until they are tender and drain.

Use the chestnuts according to the recipe – usually they are worked through a food mill or mashed with a potato masher, then sieved to form chestnut purée. This purée freezes well.

Chamonix

2 lb chestnuts
¼ cup sugar
½ cup water
½ cup unsalted butter
1½ cups heavy cream, stiffly whipped
1 teaspoon sugar
½ teaspoon vanilla
4 sponge cupcakes
2 tablespoons rum

To decorate
a few candied violets and rose petals or cherries
leaves of angelica (optional)

6 inch springform pan; pastry bag and star tube

Serves 6–8 people.

Method
Skin, cook, sieve the chestnuts to a purée and cool. Dissolve the ¼ cup sugar in the water, boil for 1 minute and cool.

To make the purée, beat the sugar syrup into the sieved chestnuts. Cream the butter thoroughly, add to the chestnut mixture and beat well. Fold in 2 tablespoons of the whipped cream.

Stir 1 teaspoon sugar and vanilla into the remaining cream.

Cut the cupcakes in half, lay them in the springform pan and moisten with rum. Press in well with a fork and leave a few minutes to set.

Loosen the sides of the pan and turn the soaked cupcakes onto a platter. Pile the chestnut mixture on the top, doming it well like a mountain, and smooth the sides with a metal spatula.

Put the sweetened whipped cream into the pastry bag fitted with a medium star tube and pipe over chestnut purée to cover it completely. Decorate with candied violets and rose petals or candied cherries, and angelica leaves, if you like.

Boîte au Chocolat

3 squares (3 oz) semisweet chocolate
1 lb chestnuts
2 tablespoons rum
2 teaspoons sugar
1 teaspoon vanilla
1 cup heavy cream, stiffly whipped

For sponge cake
½ cup self-rising flour
pinch of salt
3 eggs, separated
⅓ cup sugar
3 tablespoons butter

8 inch square cake pan; pastry bag and medium star tube

Method
To make chocolate squares: cut or chop chocolate into pieces and melt on a heatproof plate over a pan of hot water. With a metal spatula, work the chocolate until it is melted but not hot. Spread it evenly and thinly (about one-eighth inch thick) over an 8 inch square of wax paper and, when on the point of setting, mark into 1½–2 inch squares with a sharp knife. Leave in the refrigerator to harden completely (about 1 hour), then peel away the paper leaving separate squares.

Watchpoint: make the chocolate squares before the kitchen gets warm from baking the cake. Chocolate melts easily so keep it cool and avoid handling it as much as possible.

Grease cake pan and line base with wax paper; grease the paper. Sprinkle pan with sugar, then with flour and discard the excess. Set oven at moderate (350°F).

To make the sponge cake: sift the flour with the salt. Beat the egg yolks with the sugar until thick and light. Warm the butter in a bowl or cup over hot water until it is soft enough to pour but not oily.

Beat egg whites until they hold a stiff peak and fold them into the yolk mixture alternately with the flour in 3 batches. When the batter is almost smooth, pour in the butter and continue folding until mixed. Pour quickly into the pan and bake in heated oven for 25–30 minutes or until the cake springs back when lightly pressed with a fingertip. Turn out on a wire rack to cool. When cold, sprinkle cake with rum. Skin, cook and sieve the chestnuts to a purée.

Stir sugar and vanilla into the whipped cream and spread on sides of cake. Set it on a platter and very carefully and lightly press squares of chocolate, overlapping, around the sides. Pile alternate layers of chestnut purée and whipped cream on top of the cake, and finish by piping the last layer of cream into rosettes. Top the cake with remaining chocolate squares, if you like.

Mont Blanc

For meringue
2 egg whites
$\frac{1}{2}$ cup sugar

For chestnut purée
1 lb chestnuts
1 vanilla bean
2 tablespoons sugar
$\frac{1}{4}$ cup water

For cream filling
1 teaspoon sugar
$\frac{1}{2}$ teaspoon vanilla extract
$\frac{3}{4}$ cup heavy cream, stiffly whipped
1 egg white
$\frac{1}{2}$ square ($\frac{1}{2}$ oz) semisweet chocolate, grated

Pastry bag; $\frac{3}{8}$ inch and $\frac{1}{8}$ inch plain tubes

Method

Line a baking sheet with non-stick silicone paper and set oven at low (275°F).

To make the meringue: beat the egg whites until they hold a stiff peak, add 1 tablespoon of the sugar and continue beating 1 minute or until the mixture is glossy. Fold in the remaining sugar with a metal spoon. Spread out meringue into a 9 inch circle on the prepared baking sheet or pipe it, using pastry bag fitted with a three-eighth inch plain tube. Bake in heated oven for 1 hour or until crisp and pale golden. Cool, then peel off the paper before the meringue is cold.

To make the chestnut purée, skin the chestnuts and cook them with the vanilla bean added for flavor. Remove vanilla bean, drain, reserve the liquid, sieve chestnuts to a purée and cool. Dissolve the 2 tablespoons sugar in the $\frac{1}{4}$ cup water, bring to a boil and cool. Beat this syrup into the sieved chestnuts and add 1–2 tablespoons of reserved cooking liquid to make a purée that is thick enough to pipe. Put the purée into the pastry bag fitted with a one-eighth inch plain tube.

To make the filling: add the sugar and vanilla extract to the whipped cream. Beat egg white until it holds a stiff peak, then beat lightly into whipped cream until the mixture holds a shape.

Pipe chestnut purée around the edge of the meringue to form a nest. Fill the center with the whipped cream mixture and sprinkle with grated chocolate.

Chocolate and Chestnut Cake

3 squares (3 oz) semisweet chocolate, chopped
$\frac{3}{4}$ lb chestnuts
$\frac{1}{4}$ cup water
4 large eggs, separated
1 cup sugar

For filling
3 squares (3 oz) semisweet chocolate, chopped
3 tablespoons water
2 egg yolks
1 cup heavy cream, stiffly whipped
1 tablespoon sugar (or to taste)
1 tablespoon rum (or to taste)

Two 9 inch round cake pans

Method

Grease the pans. Line each base with a circle of silicone or wax paper and grease again. Set oven at moderate (350°F).

Skin, cook and sieve the chestnuts to a purée and measure them – there should be 1$\frac{1}{2}$ cups purée.

Melt 3 squares chocolate in $\frac{1}{4}$ cup water in the top of a double boiler, then cook, stirring, to a very thick cream. Cool. Beat egg yolks with 1 cup sugar until thick and light, then stir in the cooled chocolate. Beat egg whites until they hold a stiff peak and fold into the chocolate mixture alternately with the chestnut purée. Spoon half the mixture into each cake pan and bake in the heated oven for 35–40 minutes or until the cakes start to shrink from the sides of the pans. Cool 5 minutes, then turn out carefully and cool on a wire rack.

To make the filling: melt 3 oz chocolate in the water in the top of a double boiler. When very hot, take from the heat, beat in the egg yolks, one at a time, and leave to cool. Fold cooled chocolate mixture into the whipped cream with sugar and rum to taste. The mixture looks best if it is left rather streaky.

Sandwich the cakes with half the chocolate cream and spread the rest on top.

Turinois

2 lb chestnuts
1 vanilla bean
8 squares (8 oz) semisweet chocolate, chopped
$\frac{3}{4}$ cup water
$\frac{3}{4}$ cup unsalted butter
$\frac{2}{3}$ cup sugar
1 teaspoon vanilla or 1 tablespoon brandy
$\frac{3}{4}$ cup heavy cream, stiffly whipped (for serving)

Medium loaf pan (8$\frac{1}{2}$ X 4$\frac{1}{2}$ X 2$\frac{1}{2}$ inches)

Method
Lightly oil the loaf pan, line bottom with wax paper and oil the paper. Skin the chestnuts; cook them with the vanilla bean for flavor. Remove vanilla bean, drain, sieve nuts to a purée and cool.

Put the chocolate in a pan with the water, melt over gentle heat and cook, stirring, to a smooth cream. Cool.

Cream the butter in a bowl, gradually beat in the sugar and beat until light and soft. Stir in cooled chocolate with chestnut purée and flavor with vanilla or brandy. Fill prepared pan with the mixture, cover with foil and chill overnight or for up to 3 days.

Just before serving, turn out and cut in thin slices. Serve a bowl of whipped cream separately.

Ma'amoul

2 cups flour
$\frac{1}{2}$ cup unsalted butter
2 teaspoons orange flower water or rose water
1–2 tablespoons water
confectioners' sugar (for sprinkling)

For filling
$\frac{1}{3}$ cup finely chopped walnuts, almonds or pistachios
$\frac{1}{4}$–$\frac{1}{2}$ cup sugar
1 teaspoon ground cinnamon

Ma'amoul are one of the dozens of little rich pastries made famous by the Turks. Like many Middle Eastern dishes, they should be flavored with orange flower or rose water, which can be found in specialty stores and a few pharmacies. If necessary, substitute 1 teaspoon vanilla and increase the quantity of water in the recipe by 1 teaspoon.

Ma'amoul are deliciously soft and melting and they keep well in an airtight jar. Makes about 20–24 cookies.

Method
To make the dough: sift the flour into a large bowl and make a well in the center. Melt the butter, cool it and pour into the flour with the orange flower or rose water and the water. Work the mixture to a smooth dough that holds together well and chill 30 minutes.

Set oven at moderately low (325°F).

To make the filling: mix the chopped nuts with $\frac{1}{4}$–$\frac{1}{2}$ cup sugar, depending on your taste, and the cinnamon.

Roll the dough into walnut-sized balls and press a hollow in the center of each with a finger. Enlarge this to a cup shape and fill with 1 teaspoon of nut filling. Fold the dough over the top and pinch to seal it. Place the balls, sealed side down, on a baking sheet and make little indentations on the surface with a fork or with tweezers. This helps the confectioners' sugar to cling to the cookies after they are baked.

Bake cookies in heated oven for 20–25 minutes but do not let them brown. Remove and cool them – they will harden on cooling. When cold, roll the cookies in confectioners' sugar.

Marzipan Dates

Remove pits from dessert dates by making a slit along one side and lifting out the pit with the point of a knife.

Roll marzipan with your hands into a tube about $\frac{1}{2}$ inch thick and cut off even-sized pieces with a knife. Shape into ovals, press a blanched whole almond in the middle and insert the marzipan into each date. Roll in granulated sugar and wrap each date in wax paper or foil and store in an airtight container.

Marzipan Walnuts or Pecans

Roll marzipan into walnut-sized balls and press a walnut or pecan half on each side; wrap and store as for marzipan dates.

Amaretti

1 cup homemade or $\frac{1}{2}$ lb commercial almond paste
1 cup granulated sugar
2 egg whites
$\frac{1}{2}$ cup pine nuts

These famous Italian cookies are sold in many Italian stores, but they are incomparably better when baked at home. Makes about 20 cookies.

Method
Set oven at moderately low (325°F).

Cut almond paste into small pieces, add sugar and egg whites and work with your hand to form a smooth paste. Roll into walnut-sized balls and place on a greased baking sheet, leaving space between each one.

Flatten each ball slightly and sprinkle generously with pine nuts. Bake in heated oven for 15–20 minutes or until the cookies are very pale golden. Cool on a wire rack. Wrap pairs of amaretti in 2 inch squares of colored tissue paper.

Almond Paste

For 4 cup (2 lb) quantity: blanch and remove skins from 1 lb almonds. Work almonds twice through the fine blade of a grinder or work them in a blender. Mix thoroughly with 1 lb sifted confectioners' sugar. Add 1 teaspoon almond extract.

Very slightly beat 3 egg whites and stir into almond mixture to make a firm paste; knead 5 minutes with the hands to draw out the oil in the almonds.

Serve amaretti wrapped in colorful squares of tissue paper

Almond or Pecan Balls

- $\frac{3}{4}$ cup whole blanched almonds or pecans, ground
- 1 cup butter
- $\frac{1}{2}$ cup sugar
- 1 teaspoon vanilla
- pinch of salt
- 2 cups flour
- $\frac{1}{2}$ cup whole blanched almonds, or $\frac{1}{4}$ cup chopped pecans

Makes about 36 cookies.

Method

Cream butter and beat in sugar until light and fluffy. Stir in ground nuts and vanilla, sift in salt and flour and work to a smooth dough. Chill 30 minutes or until firm.

Set the oven at moderate (350°F).

Divide the dough and roll into 1 inch balls. Press a whole almond into the top of each cookie or roll in ground pecans and set on a greased baking sheet. Bake in heated oven for 15–20 minutes or until cookies are cream-colored (and the almonds on top are brown). Remove from baking sheet carefully as cookies are delicate when still hot.

Pecan Fruit Cake

- 5 cups coarsely chopped pecans
- 2 cups butter
- 2 cups sugar
- 6 eggs, separated
- 3 cups cake flour
- $\frac{1}{2}$ teaspoon salt
- 1 cup candied cherries
- $\frac{1}{3}$ cup coarsely chopped candied pineapple
- 1 teaspoon vanilla

10 inch tube pan

Method

Grease pan and set oven at low (300°F).

Cream the butter and beat in the sugar until the mixture is light and fluffy. Beat in the egg yolks, one at a time, and continue beating 2 minutes. Sift flour with salt, add one-third to the candied fruits and nuts and toss well so that they are coated. Stir the flour, then the fruits and nuts with the vanilla into butter mixture with lemon extract.

Beat egg whites until they hold a stiff peak and fold into cake mixture as lightly as possible. Spoon batter into the prepared pan and bake in heated oven for $1\frac{1}{2}$ hours or until a skewer inserted in the center of the cake comes out clean. Let cake cool in the pan. It will improve in flavor and texture if kept in an air-tight container for 1 month or more.

Walnut Bread

- $\frac{1}{2}$ cup coarsely chopped walnuts
- $\frac{1}{2}$ cup sugar
- $\frac{1}{2}$ cup golden syrup or honey
- $\frac{3}{4}$ cup milk
- $\frac{1}{3}$ cup golden raisins
- 2 cups flour
- pinch of salt
- 3 teaspoons baking powder
- 1 egg, beaten to mix

Medium loaf pan ($8\frac{1}{2}$ X $4\frac{1}{2}$ X $2\frac{1}{2}$ inches)

Method

Grease loaf pan and sprinkle it with flour, discarding the excess. Set oven at moderate (350°F).

Heat the sugar, golden syrup or honey, milk and golden raisins in a saucepan and stir gently until the sugar has dissolved. Cool.

Sift the flour, salt and baking powder into a bowl, add the walnuts and make a well in the center. Stir the sugar and syrup mixture into the egg and pour into the well in the flour. Stir until smooth and pour the batter into the prepared pan. Bake in heated oven for 1 hour or until a skewer inserted in the center comes out clean. Turn out on a wire rack to cool.

Walnut bread improves if kept in an airtight container for 1–2 weeks. To serve, slice it and spread with butter.

Golden syrup is made in England as a byproduct of refining sugar. It is available in many supermarkets but if you cannot find it, honey is the best substitute.

Walnut Kisses

- 2 cups walnuts, ground
- 1 tablespoon dry instant coffee
- 2 tablespoons honey
- $\frac{1}{2}$ cup dry cocoa

Makes 18–20 cookies.

Method

Mix ground walnuts with the coffee and add enough honey to form a very stiff mixture. Cover and chill 1 hour, then shape into small balls, about 1 inch in diameter, and roll them in cocoa. Store in an airtight container.

Chocolate Walnut Sponge Cake

- $\frac{3}{4}$ cup walnuts, ground
- 4 eggs, separated
- $\frac{1}{2}$ cup sugar
- 2 tablespoons fresh white breadcrumbs (see box)
- grated rind of $\frac{1}{2}$ lemon
- 1 tablespoon rum
- $\frac{1}{2}$ cup coarsely chopped walnuts (to finish)

For frosting

- 2 squares (2 oz) semisweet chocolate
- 1 egg
- 6 tablespoons sugar
- 6 tablespoons butter

Two 8 inch cake pans

Method

Grease cake pans, line with a circle of wax paper and grease again. Set oven at moderate (350°F).

To make the cake: beat egg yolks with sugar for 5 minutes or until the mixture is light and very thick. Stir in the breadcrumbs, ground walnuts, grated lemon rind and rum. Whip egg whites until they hold a stiff peak and fold into the walnut mixture as lightly as possible. Spoon mixture into prepared pans and bake in heated oven for 20–25 minutes or until the cakes spring back when lightly pressed with a fingertip. Cool 5 minutes, then turn out and finish cooling on a wire rack.

Spread the coarsely chopped walnuts in a pan and bake in heated oven for 7–10 minutes or until browned. Cool.

To make the frosting: cut up the chocolate and melt it on a heatproof plate over a pan of hot water. Stir until smooth, then let cool.

Beat the eggs and sugar in a bowl over a pan of hot water until thick and light. Take from heat and continue beating until the mixture is cool. If using an electric beater, no heat is necessary. Cream the butter. Stir cooled chocolate into egg mixture, then beat in the butter.

Sandwich the 2 cake halves with one-third of the frosting and spread remainder over the top and sides. Sprinkle over the toasted walnuts and chill the cake thoroughly before serving.

White Breadcrumbs
The easiest way to make fresh breadcrumbs is in the blender. Cut sliced white bread into cubes, removing the crust. Reduce these to crumbs, 1–2 slices at a time, in a blender at a moderately high speed.

Honey Cakes
The flavor of all cakes and cookies made with honey improves if they are kept in an airtight container for 2–3 days.

Hazelnut Honey Cookies

½ cup shelled hazelnuts
about ¼ cup honey (for filling)
1¼ cups flour
pinch of salt
¼ cup butter
¼ cup granulated sugar
confectioners' sugar (for sprinkling)

2 inch plain cookie cutter

Makes 15–18 sandwiched cookies.

Method

Set oven at moderate (350°F).

Brown hazelnuts in the oven and rub in a cloth to remove the skins. Leave to cool, then grind them. Sift the flour with salt.

Cream the butter, beat in the sugar until light and fluffy, then work in the flour and ground hazelnuts. Knead the mixture lightly to a smooth dough and chill 30 minutes or until firm.

Roll out the dough to one-eighth inch thickness and cut into rounds with the cutter. Line a baking sheet with silicone paper or foil, place cookies on it and bake in heated oven for 7–8 minutes. Do not let the cookies brown or they will taste bitter. Remove them from the baking sheet all at once by carefully sliding them off the paper or foil (this prevents cookies left on the sheet from over-browning). Cool on a wire rack.

When cold, sandwich the cookies with honey and sprinkle generously with confectioners' sugar.

Turquois (Almond Meringue and Chocolate Gâteau)

For Japonais meringue
4 egg whites
1 cup whole blanched almonds, ground
1 cup sugar

For chocolate meringue mousse
4 squares (4 oz) semisweet chocolate, chopped
¼ cup butter
2 egg yolks
¾ cup sugar
½ cup water
3 egg whites

To finish
cocoa (for sprinkling)
3 squares (3 oz) semisweet chocolate, grated

***Pastry bag and* ⅜ inch plain tube**

Method

Line baking sheets with silicone paper and mark three 7-inch circles on the paper. Set the oven at low (300°F).

To make the Japonais meringue: work the ground almonds and sugar through a coarse sieve. Stiffly whip the egg whites and fold in the almond mixture. Put the Japonais mixture into a pastry bag fitted with a ⅜ inch plain tube and pipe the mixture in spirals on the prepared baking sheets to form 7-inch rounds. Bake in the heated oven for 30–35 minutes or until the Japonais is brown and crisp. Let cool slightly, then carefully peel off the paper and transfer meringue rounds to a wire rack to cool completely.

To make the chocolate meringue mousse: melt the chocolate in the top of a double boiler. When almost melted, stir in the butter in small pieces until the butter is melted. Take from the heat, beat in the egg yolks and let cool. In a saucepan heat the sugar with the water until dissolved, bring to a boil and boil until the syrup forms a thread between finger and thumb when a little is lifted on a spoon (234°F on a sugar thermometer).

Stiffly whip the egg whites, gradually add the hot syrup, beating constantly, and continue beating until this meringue is cool. Fold the meringue into the chocolate mixture.

Sandwich the Japonais meringue rounds with half the chocolate mousse mixture and spread the remaining mousse on the top and sides of the turquois. Sprinkle the top with cocoa and press grated chocolate around the sides. With the point of a knife, mark the top of the turquois in a lattice pattern.

KINDS OF NUTS

Nuts have always been plentiful and popular in North America. Raw, cooked, fried, roasted or ground, the list of nuts that give great cooking and eating pleasure is long. The following are some of the most plentiful.

Almonds

These add texture and flavor in cooking and baking. Almonds have a particular affinity for fish, seafood and chicken and are a classic garnish for vegetables such as green beans and cauliflower.

Many desserts, fine coffee-cakes, cookies and candies depend on almonds for their characteristic soft texture and fragrant taste.

Brazil Nuts

These are really not nuts at all but the edible seeds of a fruit grown in South America. Whole Brazil nuts are eaten plain, salted or sugared. Chopped or sliced, they are interesting in pilaf, cakes and fruitcake, breads, pastry and stuffing for chicken.

Butternuts

Native to North America and used primarily in cakes and cookies, butternuts are available only in the areas in which they are grown, namely from New Brunswick to Georgia and the Dakotas and Arkansas.

Cashews

Kidney-shaped, creamy white and sweet, the cashews here come mainly from India. They are excellent eaten plain or salted and add flavor and texture to curries, many casserole dishes, salads, desserts and candies.

Chestnuts

Available fresh from early fall to the beginning of spring, chestnuts can also be bought canned (in sweetened or unsweetened form), whole or puréed, in syrup or glazed. They are used in desserts as an elegant confection (marrons glacés). Unsweetened canned chestnuts are a good substitute for fresh chestnuts when these are not available. Sweetened chestnut purée is very rich and must be used sparingly.

Hazelnuts and Filberts

These are the same nut, except the hazelnut is wild and the filbert is cultivated. Both can be eaten out of hand and they are excellent in cakes, cookies, candies and stuffings for poultry.

Cooking with nuts

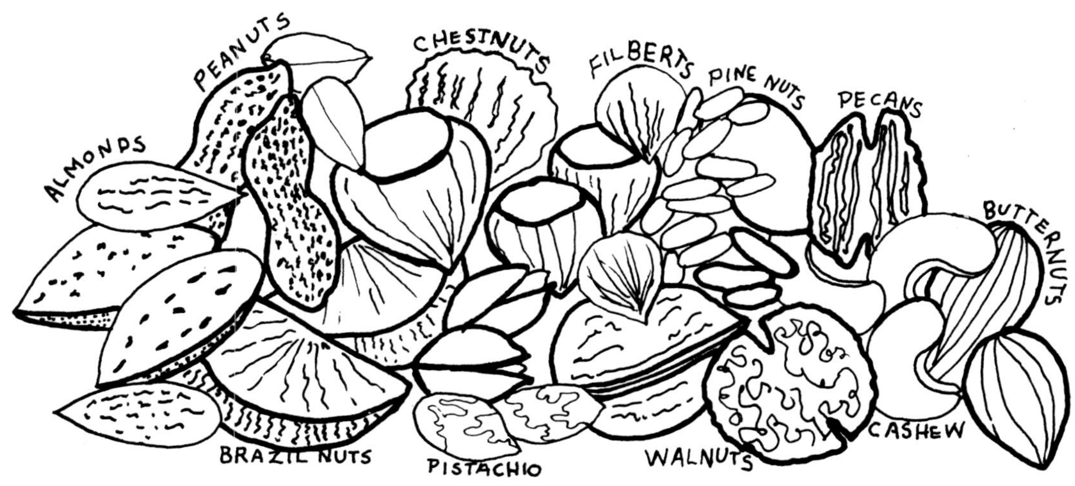

Peanuts
The most common nut, peanuts are sold in the shell or shelled, roasted and salted, made into peanut butter or peanut oil, and the shells are even used as fodder for cattle. Their use in cooking is vast, ranging from peanut soup to peanut cookies, cakes and candies.

Pecans
Indigenous to North America and closely associated with Southern cooking, pecans are excellent eaten out of hand, either plain or salted, spiced or sugared. They are equally good in pies, cakes, cookies, candies, ice cream, with vegetables and in stuffing for poultry.

Pine Nuts
Some pine nuts come from the Pacific Coast where they are known as Indian nuts, pignons or piñons. Others are from the Mediterranean area and are called pignolias when imported. Widely used in Near Eastern and Italian cooking, they give flavor to meat, rice and vegetable dishes. They are also used in sauces, salads and cookies.

Pistachio Nuts
These nuts are grown in Turkey and Iran. When soaked in brine and roasted in the sun, pistachios become deliciously salty for eating out of hand.

Roasted unsalted pistachio nutmeats are used as flavoring and coloring accents in ice cream, in cakes and candymaking and are delicious additions to pilafs, stuffings and terrines.

Walnuts
Best known in the form of the English walnut with its light tan shell that divides in half so easily, walnuts grow in temperate zones everywhere and are one of the most popular nuts for eating out of hand.

English walnuts add interest to cakes, cookies, breads, desserts and candies; young, green walnuts can be pickled. In France walnut oil is used in salads and for cooking.

The black walnut, a native American nut, has a very pronounced flavor that is either loved or loathed. It is used in cookies, candies, cakes and ice cream.

Roast turkey with oyster stuffing (recipe is on page 101) is served with sweet potatoes and broccoli

SERVE THE TRADITIONAL TURKEY FOR A HOLIDAY MENU

Potage Bonne Femme

Roast Turkey with Oyster Stuffing
Sweet Potatoes with Orange
Broccoli Spears
or
Shoulder of Lamb à la Turque
Buttered Leaf Spinach
or Spinach Purée

Coupe Française or Sherry Trifle

Red wine – Cabernet Sauvignon (California)
White wine – Chelois (Finger Lakes)

If you choose the traditional American turkey – rich and crisp and stuffed with fresh oysters and celery – a foreign wine seems out of order, so choose a native red wine. California's top red is Cabernet Sauvignon, particularly good when from a premium vineyard near San Francisco.

Or if you choose the shoulder of lamb, be assured that the wines from the cabernet sauvignon grape have long been regarded as ideal for lamb.

If you prefer a white wine with turkey, the new French-American grape varieties are yielding wines like Chelois that are worthy of the occasion. If you happen to live in one of the other wine-producing states, like Ohio, Maryland or Washington, this might be the time to give the local vintages a try.

TIMETABLE

Day before
Make stock for turkey gravy *or lamb.* Make soup, sieve or blend it and refrigerate. Cut and fry croûtons and keep in a plastic bag. *Prepare stuffing for lamb and refrigerate.*

Morning
Make coupe Française, pour into glasses, cover with plastic wrap and refrigerate. *Or prepare sherry trifle, omitting decorations, cover and refrigerate.*
Prepare oyster stuffing and cool; stuff turkey not more than 3 hours before cooking; coat skin with butter, wrap in foil and refrigerate.
Stuff lamb, cover securely and refrigerate.
Boil sweet potatoes. Leave in pan ready for glazing.
Prepare broccoli *or wash spinach.*
Prepare garnish for lamb and cover.
Prepare liaison for soup but do not add.
Prepare leek garnish and cover.

Assemble equipment for final cooking from 3:45 or 4:45 for dinner around 8 p.m.

You will find that **cooking times** given in the individual recipes for these dishes have sometimes been adapted in the timetable to help you when cooking and serving this menu as a party meal.

Order of Work

3:45 or **4:45**
Set oven for turkey (time depends on size of bird).
4:00 or **5:00**
Put in turkey to roast.
5:30
Baste turkey. *Set oven for lamb.*
5:45
Put in lamb to roast.
6:15
Baste turkey *or lamb.*
Decorate sherry trifle.
7:15
Baste turkey *or lamb.*
Garnish coupe Française and chill.
Put sweet potatoes in oven and baste.
7:30
Cook broccoli *or spinach* and drain.
7:45
Reheat soup gently.
Transfer turkey to serving platter; turn down oven and keep turkey warm; make gravy.
Transfer lamb to platter; turn down oven and reheat garnishes; make lamb gravy; arrange prunes around lamb; arrange tomato garnish on separate dish and keep everything hot.
Heat croûtons. Add liaison to soup but do not let it boil.
8:00
Serve soup.
Reheat broccoli *or spinach* in butter and transfer to serving dish.

Potage bonne femme, a creamy leek and potato soup, is served with croûtons separately

Appetizer

Potage Bonne Femme

6–8 medium leeks
3 medium potatoes, peeled and sliced
5 tablespoons butter
salt and pepper
2 cups milk
2 cups water
2 egg yolks
$\frac{3}{4}$ cup light cream
1 tablespoon chopped parsley (for garnish)
croûtons (for serving)

Method
Trim and discard the roots and green tops from the leeks. Reserve 1 leek for garnish, split the remainder lengthwise, wash well and slice the white part.

Melt the butter in a large saucepan, add the leeks and potatoes with seasoning and cook over low heat, stirring, until they are almost soft. Cover with foil and the lid and cook 10 minutes or until very soft. Pour in the milk and water and stir until mixture comes to a boil. Half cover with the lid and simmer 15 minutes.
Watchpoint: do not boil hard or the soup will curdle.

Work the soup through a sieve or food mill or purée it in a blender.

Cut the reserved leek into fine slices, put in cold water, bring to a boil and boil 2 minutes. Drain and pat dry with paper towels.

Reheat the soup; mix the egg yolks and cream in a bowl and stir in a little of the hot soup. Pour the mixture back into the remaining soup and stir over low heat until the soup thickens slightly.
Watchpoint: do not let the soup boil or it will curdle.

Garnish the soup with a little sliced leek and chopped parsley. Serve the croûtons separately.

Croûtons
Cut several slices of bread into cubes, removing the crusts. Fry the cubes in 3–4 tablespoons hot shallow fat or in deep fat until golden brown; drain on paper towels. Sprinkle lightly with salt.

Entrée

Roast Turkey with Oyster Stuffing

6–8 lb turkey
salt and pepper
$\frac{1}{2}$ cup butter, softened

For oyster stuffing
1 pint shucked oysters, drained
1 large onion, finely chopped
$\frac{1}{2}$ cup butter
3 cups fresh white breadcrumbs
3 stalks of celery, chopped
1 teaspoon mixed herbs (thyme, savory, oregano)
1 tablespoon chopped parsley
milk or water (to bind)

For gravy
1–1$\frac{1}{2}$ cups stock, made from turkey giblets (except liver), root vegetables, bouquet garni, seasoning
1 teaspoon arrowroot or cornstarch (mixed to a paste with 1 tablespoon water) – optional

Trussing needle and string or poultry pins

This recipe uses the slow roasting method of cooking turkey in foil. For regular and French roasting methods, see Volume 8.

Method
Set oven at moderately low (325°F).

To make the oyster stuffing: cook onion in butter until golden, add about one-third of the breadcrumbs and stir over heat until all the butter is absorbed. Transfer the mixture to a bowl and add remaining crumbs, celery, herbs and plenty of seasoning. Drain the oysters, chop them lightly, add to the mixture and stir in enough milk or water to bind the stuffing.

Wipe the cavity of the turkey with a damp cloth and rub the inside with about $\frac{1}{2}$ teaspoon salt. Stuff the bird and truss it with string or secure with poultry pins.

Rub the skin of the bird with softened butter and wrap in foil. Roast in heated oven for 2$\frac{1}{2}$–3$\frac{1}{2}$ hours (170°F on a meat thermometer inserted in the thigh) or until the juice that runs from the thickest part of the thigh is clear, not pink, when pierced with a skewer.

Unwrap the bird for the last 20 minutes and increase the heat to hot (400°F) so it browns. Pour any juices from the foil into the roasting pan for the gravy.

Transfer the turkey to a platter, remove the trussing strings or poultry pins and keep warm. Pour off the fat from the roasting pan, leaving sediment behind, and deglaze the pan with stock. Bring to a boil, boil 5 minutes or until the flavor is concentrated and thicken, if you like, by stirring in the arrowroot or cornstarch paste. Bring the gravy just to a boil, taste for seasoning and strain into a sauce boat.

Serve the turkey with sweet potatoes with orange, and buttered broccoli spears.

For oyster stuffing, mix the onion, breadcrumbs, celery and herbs together before adding the drained, chopped oysters

After stuffing and trussing the turkey, rub the skin with softened butter, wrap in foil and put it in the roasting pan

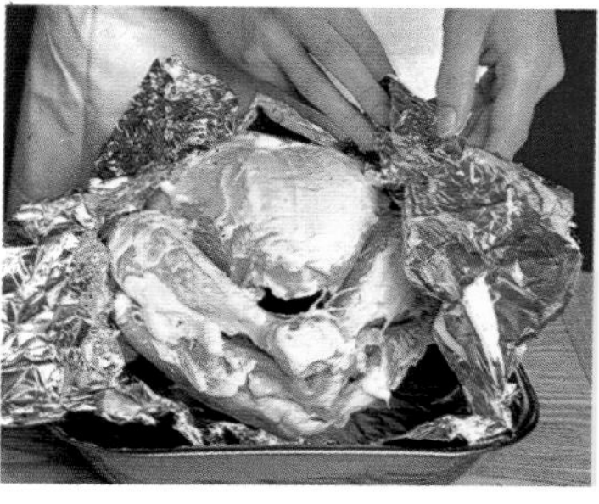

Accompaniment to entrée

Sweet Potatoes with Orange

4 large sweet potatoes, peeled
1 tablespoon grated orange rind
$\frac{1}{2}$ cup orange juice
6 tablespoons butter
$\frac{1}{4}$ cup brown sugar
salt and pepper

Method
Set the oven at moderately hot (375°F).

Cut the potatoes in quarters and trim away the corners. Cook in boiling water for 15 minutes or until tender. Drain them thoroughly.

In a pan melt the butter and sugar with the orange rind, juice and seasoning and spoon over the potatoes in a baking dish. Bake in heated oven, basting and turning them often, for 15–20 minutes or until the potatoes are glazed and brown.

Shoulder of lamb à la Turque is garnished with stuffed tomato halves and prunes stuffed with chutney

Alternative entrée

Shoulder of Lamb à la Turque

4–5 lb shoulder of lamb, boned (bones reserved)
salt and pepper
1–2 cloves of garlic, peeled and cut in slivers
6 tablespoons butter
1 teaspoon rosemary

For stuffing
2 tablespoons butter
1 medium onion, finely chopped
1 cup (½ lb) chicken livers, coarsely chopped
½ cup rice, boiled and well drained
1 tablespoon chopped parsley
1 teaspoon marjoram or thyme
½ cup raisins
2 egg yolks (to bind)

For gravy
1–1½ cups stock (made from the bones with root vegetables and seasoning)
1–2 teaspoons flour
1 teaspoon tomato paste

For garnish
10–12 large prunes, soaked according to package directions
½ cup stock
⅓ cup raisins
2 medium onions, sliced
3 tablespoons butter
4 medium tomatoes, peeled, halved and seeded
black pepper, freshly ground
1–2 tablespoons chutney

Trussing needle and string or poultry pins

Method

Sprinkle the cut surface of the lamb with salt and pepper.

To make the stuffing: melt the butter, add the onion and sauté until it is golden. Add the chicken livers and cook briskly, turning them frequently, until browned. Transfer the mixture to a bowl and combine with the rice, herbs, raisins and egg yolks.

Season well and spoon the stuffing into the lamb. Sew up the opening with a trussing needle and string or secure with poultry pins, keeping the meat in the original shape as much as possible.

Set the oven at moderately hot (375°F).

Make several incisions on the outside of the meat with the point of a knife and push in slivers of garlic. Coat it thickly with butter, sprinkle with rosemary and roast the lamb in heated oven, basting often, for 1½–2 hours or until a meat thermometer inserted in the meat (not stuffing) registers 160°F (for medium done meat).

To prepare the garnish: simmer the prunes in the stock until tender, then remove the pits. Soak the raisins in hot water to cover for about 30 minutes, then drain and pat dry with paper towels. Fry the onions in half the butter until soft, add the raisins and continue frying until the onions are browned.

Place tomato halves on a baking sheet and dot with remaining butter. Season with salt and black pepper and heat in the oven with the lamb for 2–3 minutes.

Arrange the raisin and onion mixture on each tomato half and stuff the prunes with chutney. Keep the garnish warm.

Transfer the lamb to a warm platter and remove the trussing strings or poultry pins.

To make the gravy: discard fat from the roasting pan, leaving sediment. Stir in the flour and cook, stirring, until lightly browned. Add the stock and tomato paste; bring to a boil, stirring constantly, simmer 2 minutes, taste for seasoning and strain.

Surround the lamb with the stuffed prunes and spoon over a little of the gravy, serving the rest in a gravy boat. Serve with a garnish of tomato halves and stuffed prunes and creamed spinach or buttered leaf spinach.

Accompaniment to entrée

Creamed Spinach

1–1½ lb fresh spinach or 1 package frozen spinach
1 tablespoon butter
2–3 tablespoons heavy cream
pinch of nutmeg
salt and pepper (to taste)

Method

Wash the spinach thoroughly and cook it in boiling salted water for 5 minutes or until it is just tender. Or cook frozen spinach according to the package instructions.

Drain spinach and press it well with a spoon or plate to remove as much water as possible.

Work the spinach through a sieve or purée it in a blender.

Coupe Française is topped with a pyramid of cherries or strawberries just before serving

Dessert

Coupe Française

$1\frac{1}{2}$ cups milk
1 envelope gelatin
$\frac{1}{4}$ cup cold water
thinly peeled rind of 1 lemon
4 egg yolks
$\frac{1}{4}$ cup sugar
1 teaspoon vanilla
$\frac{3}{4}$ cup heavy cream
2 egg whites

To finish
1 can (16 oz) cherries in syrup, drained or 1 pint fresh strawberries, hulled and sprinkled with 1 tablespoon sugar

4 coupe or sherbet glasses

Method
Sprinkle the gelatin over the water in a small container and let stand 5 minutes or until spongy.

Scald the milk with the lemon rind, cover and leave to infuse 10 minutes. Beat the egg yolks and sugar together until thick and light. Gradually stir the hot milk into the egg yolk mixture, then strain it back into the pan. Cook the mixture over low heat, stirring constantly, until the custard coats the back of a spoon.

Watchpoint: do not let the custard boil or it will curdle.

Take from heat and stir in the softened gelatin until dissolved.

Cool the custard, then stir in the vanilla and cream. Beat the egg whites until they hold a stiff peak. Stand the custard over a bowl of ice water and stir gently until it begins to thicken.

Fold the egg whites gently into the custard. Pour into coupe or sherbet glasses and chill 1–2 hours until set.

To serve, arrange the cherries or strawberries in a pyramid on top of each coupe. Serve very cold.

For coupe Française, gently fold the stiffly beaten egg whites into the custard, cream and vanilla mixture

Alternative dessert

Sherry Trifle

7 inch sponge cake or 6 cupcakes (see Volume 6)
$\frac{1}{2}$ cup raspberry or strawberry jam or 1 package frozen raspberries (thawed)
$\frac{1}{4}$ cup sherry or fruit juice
2 cups vanilla custard sauce (made with 2 cups milk, 3 tablespoons sugar, $\frac{1}{2}$ teaspoon vanilla and 4 egg yolks)

For decoration
1 cup heavy cream, whipped until it holds a soft shape
candied cherries, halved
candied angelica, cut into leaves

Pastry bag and medium star tube

Fruit juice may be substituted for the sherry in this recipe, if you like.

Method
Split the sponge cake or cupcakes, sandwich with jam, cut the cakes into chunks and arrange in the bottom of a glass bowl. If using raspberries, cut the cake into chunks, arrange half in the bowl, spoon over the raspberries and add the remaining cake. Spoon over the sherry or fruit juice.

To make vanilla custard sauce: put the milk in a pan with the sugar and vanilla. Beat the egg yolks in a bowl until light-colored. Scald the vanilla-flavored milk and gradually stir into the egg yolks. Return to pan and stir with a wooden spoon over gentle heat until the custard coats the back of a spoon and looks creamy; strain it back into the bowl.

Watchpoint: if the custard becomes too hot and starts to curdle, pour it at once into the bowl without straining and whisk briskly for about 10 seconds.

While the custard is still hot, pour it over the cake. Sprinkle with a little extra sugar to help prevent a skin from forming, and chill until set.

Spread a little cream over the top of the custard. Stiffly whip the rest, spoon it into the pastry bag fitted with the star tube and pipe a lattice pattern on top of the trifle with rosettes around the edge. Decorate with candied cherries and angelica leaves.

Sauerkraut soup, with sausage, is a typical Polish dish (recipe is on page 108)

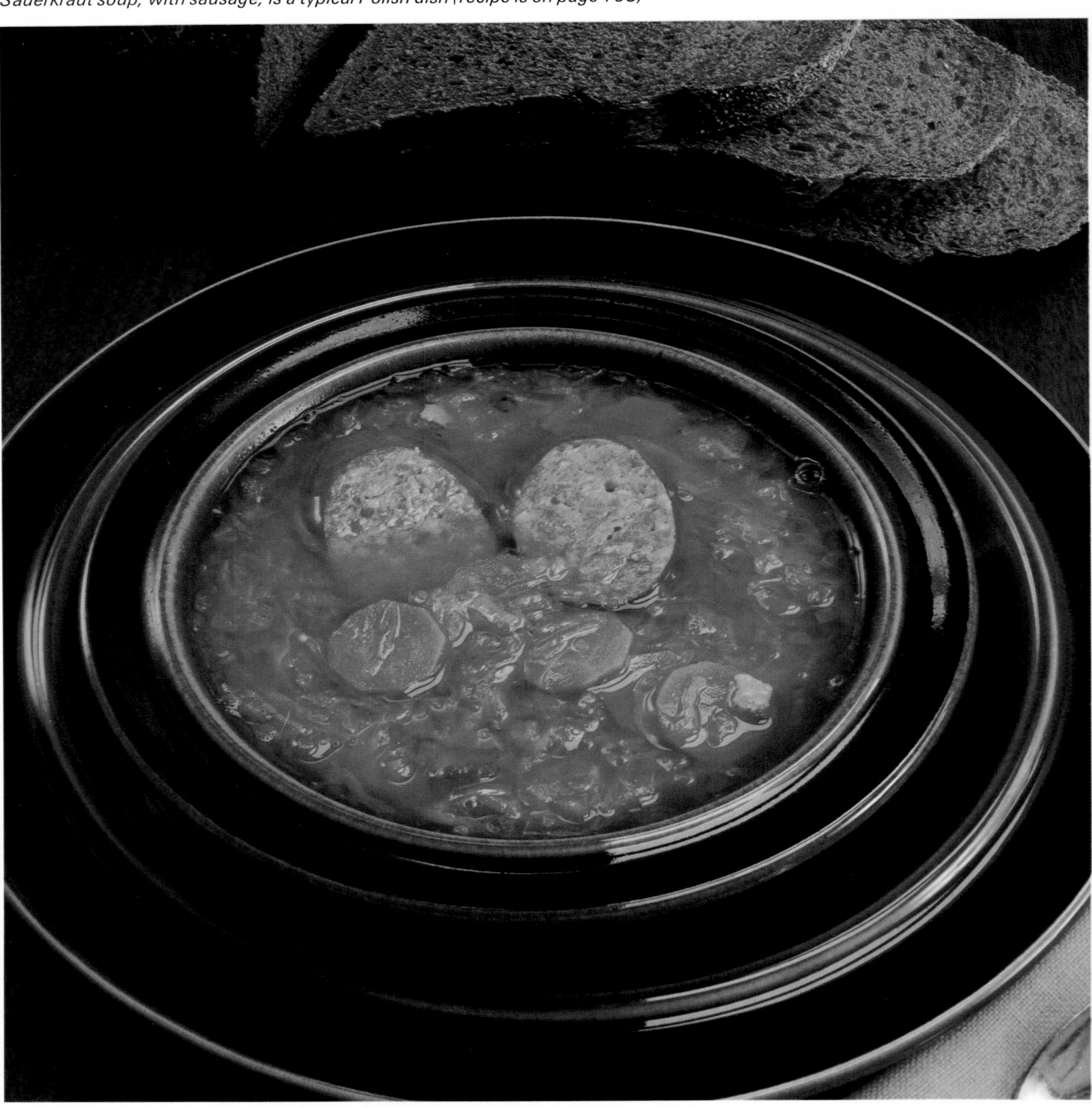

CENTRAL EUROPEAN COOKING

Central Europeans dress their foods as imaginatively as they dress themselves in costumes of striking colors and patterns. The glowing scarlet of paprika and peppers, the rich crimson of beet and the white of sour cream are typical ingredients in the cooking of Hungary, Poland, Czechoslovakia and Yugoslavia.

Wars and nature have conspired over the centuries to keep Central Europe poor so that simple, filling soups, thick stews, breads and pastries are standard diet; this simplicity, however, is far from dull.

The quality of many local products – paprika and flour from Hungary, pork and mushrooms from Poland and Czechoslovakian beer – is remarkable, and with French, Turkish and Balkan influences, it is not surprising that some dishes contain exotic spices and seasonings. The Czechs and Hungarians cook their meat with fruits and the Poles add fruit to soups to give the tart, bracing flavor that startles Anglo-Saxons familiar only with sweet fruit desserts.

Fish are popular and since much of the region is inland, most fish come from fresh water. Cabbage, potatoes and barley are everywhere and Hungarians like their homemade noodles so much that sometimes they add sugar and serve them as a dessert.

Quite a few Central European dishes are made with butter, eggs, sour cream and yogurt and this is not surprising since households in rural areas churn their own butter from the abundant fresh cream. Fresh eggs are equally plentiful and are common ingredients in innumerable dishes.

All Central European and Eastern countries share a passion for pastries. Some are adapted from Turkish pastries, but many, like the popular layered torte and the famous strudels, are characteristic of the area.

The following recipes give a taste of some Central European dishes and prove that although the extravagant banquets given by Hungarian and Polish aristocrats are part of the past, the tradition of good food remains.

Bill Rice, author of our feature on Central European cooking, trained at L'Ecole du Cordon Bleu in Paris.

Now 'Style' food coordinator of 'The Washington Post', Bill has traveled extensively throughout Central Europe and says, 'Central Europeans have perfected one of the most difficult cooking arts, combining simple ingredients to produce exotic tastes.'

The following two herring dishes have many of the same ingredients. The salad is served cold in Hungary as an appetizer and the casserole is served hot in Poland as a main course.

Herring Casserole

2 small salted herring
4 large potatoes, peeled and sliced
2–3 tablespoons browned breadcrumbs
4 hard-cooked eggs, sliced
2 tablespoons melted butter
salt and pepper
$\frac{1}{3}$ cup sour cream

Method

Soak the herring in cold water for 8 hours, changing the water each hour. Dry the fish, cut away the flesh, discarding skin and bones, and chop it.

Boil potatoes for 10 minutes or until just tender; drain, dry and combine them with the herring.

Butter a baking dish and sprinkle the inside with some of the breadcrumbs. Line the bottom with a layer of potatoes and herring, then add a layer of sliced egg. Spoon over some sour cream and season lightly. Repeat the layers, ending with potatoes and herring.

Sprinkle the mixture with the remaining breadcrumbs and melted butter. Cover and bake in a moderately hot oven (375°F) for 35–40 minutes or until browned.

Herring Salad

2 small pickled herring, sliced or 1 jar (8 oz) sliced pickled herring
2 hard-cooked eggs, chopped
2 large boiled potatoes, diced
1 tablespoon fresh dill, chopped
2 small apples, pared, cored and diced
2 tablespoons finely chopped onion
salt and pepper
$\frac{1}{2}$ cup sour cream
1 tablespoon chopped parsley

Method

Combine all the ingredients in a salad bowl with seasoning to taste and add the sour cream. Mix well, cover and chill 1–3 hours.

Sprinkle the salad with chopped parsley before serving.

Sauerkraut Soup

1 lb fresh or canned sauerkraut
1 cup water (if using fresh sauerkraut)
2 quarts beef stock
2 slices of bacon, diced
1 medium onion, coarsely chopped
1 carrot, finely sliced
1 tablespoon flour
1 teaspoon sweet red paprika
$\frac{1}{2}$ lb Polish sausage or frankfurters, cut in $\frac{1}{2}$ inch pieces
1 bay leaf
8–10 peppercorns (tied in a piece of cheesecloth)
salt and pepper
1 teaspoon sugar (optional)

For garnish
2 slices of bacon, diced, fried until crisp and drained (optional)

In Poland this soup is served at a late evening supper. It is said to be an excellent counter to the possible after-effects of alcohol.

Method

Chop the sauerkraut finely. If fresh, drain it and bring to a boil in 1 cup water and simmer 45 minutes. If canned, bring it to a boil in its own juices and simmer 10 minutes. Drain, reserving the liquid.

Heat the sauerkraut with the stock and keep warm.

In a frying pan cook the bacon until crisp. Remove it, and fry the onion and carrot in the fat until they begin to brown. Add the flour, paprika and Polish sausage or frankfurters and cook gently for 3 minutes, stirring.

Slowly pour the reserved sauerkraut liquid into the frying pan, stirring constantly. When the mixture is blended and thick, stir into the sauerkraut mixture. Add the diced bacon, bay leaf and peppercorns; stir well and simmer 15–20 minutes. After 10 minutes, taste the soup, season and, if it is too tart, add 1 teaspoon of sugar.

Serve in large bowls garnished with pieces of fried bacon, if you like, and pass dark rye bread and butter.

Caraway Seed Soup

2 tablespoons caraway seeds
2 tablespoons butter
2 tablespoons flour
5 cups beef stock
salt and pepper

For garnish
2–3 slices of white bread, crusts removed, cut in cubes and fried in 3–4 tablespoons oil and butter, mixed (for croûtons)

Method

In a heavy saucepan melt the butter. Add the flour and caraway seeds and stir over medium heat until lightly browned. It is this browning that gives flavor to the soup.

Add the stock and seasoning to taste. Stir well, bring to a boil and simmer gently 15–20 minutes.

Fry the croûtons until golden brown and drain them on paper towels.

Sprinkle half the croûtons on top of the soup and serve the rest separately.

Baked carp is placed on a bed of sliced potatoes and covered with sour cream and paprika

Baked Whole Carp

4 lb whole carp, cleaned and scaled
2 slices of bacon
4–5 medium potatoes
$\frac{1}{4}$ cup butter
salt
1 tablespoon sweet red paprika
1 tablespoon flour
pinch of white pepper
1 cup sour cream

For garnish
$\frac{1}{4}$ cup chopped parsley
sweet red paprika (for sprinkling)

River carp is called for in this traditional Serbian dish from Yugoslavia, but you can substitute sea bass, red snapper or cod.

Method

Wash the fish and pat dry with paper towels; make sure all the intestines and scales are removed. Using a sharp knife make parallel incisions, each $1\frac{1}{2}$ inches long, along one side of the fish from head to tail. Cut the slices of bacon into strips, then place them in the incisions.

Cook the potatoes in boiling salted water for 5 minutes; peel and cut in $\frac{1}{4}$ inch slices.

Set oven at moderately low (325°F).

Butter a deep baking dish large enough to hold the fish without touching the sides. Line the bottom with potato slices and season lightly with salt and half the paprika.

Insert a rack into the baking dish above the potatoes and place the fish on it, bacon side up. Dot the fish with the remaining butter. Mix flour with $\frac{1}{2}$ teaspoon salt and a pinch of white pepper.

Bake the fish in the heated oven for 10 minutes. Sprinkle on the flour and remaining paprika, and season. Bake for 10 minutes longer. Spoon half of the sour cream over the fish and raise oven temperature to moderate (350°F). After 10–15 minutes, add the rest of the sour cream and cook 5–7 minutes longer or until the fish flakes easily.

Take the dish from the oven and remove the rack carefully with the fish on it. Place the fish on the bed of potatoes, top potatoes with chopped parsley, sprinkle fish with paprika and serve in baking dish. To serve: with a sharp knife, cut the fish into steaks through the backbone.

Fish in Black Sauce

1½ lb red snapper or other firm fish fillets
2 tablespoons butter
2 carrots, diced
2 stalks of celery, diced
1 medium onion, finely chopped
salt
black pepper, freshly ground
1 bay leaf
½ teaspoon dried thyme
2–3 sprigs of parsley
1–1¼ cups dark beer
1 cup red wine
3 tablespoons lemon juice or wine vinegar
2 teaspoons sugar
¼ cup chopped walnuts
¼ cup seedless raisins
2 tablespoons plum jam
¼ cup whole blanched almonds, chopped (to finish)

Method

In a large flameproof casserole, melt the butter, add the carrot, celery and onion and cook 5 minutes or until soft. Add the seasonings and herbs, then add 1 cup beer, the wine, lemon juice or vinegar, sugar, walnuts, raisins and jam. Mix well and simmer 15 minutes. Add more beer if the sauce mixture is too thick.

Lay the fish fillets in a skillet or buttered baking dish, spoon over the sauce and poach on top of the stove or in a moderate oven (350°F) for 12–15 minutes or until the fish is just tender.

Arrange the fish on a platter, spoon the sauce on top, discarding the bay leaf, and sprinkle with almonds.

Summer Squash in Dill and Sour Cream

1½ lb summer squash, peeled and cut in cubes
1 tablespoon chopped fresh dill
¾ cup dill pickle juice, warmed
¾ cup sour cream
1½ tablespoons butter
1½ tablespoons flour
1 tablespoon chopped parsley
salt and pepper

Method

Melt the butter in a saucepan and stir in the flour off the heat. Add the dill pickle juice and heat, stirring until the mixture thickens.

Add the squash, sour cream, fresh dill, parsley and seasoning to taste; simmer 8–10 minutes or until the squash are tender.

Carrots in Cream and Dill

8 carrots, peeled and thinly sliced
½ cup heavy cream
1 tablespoon chopped fresh dill
1 cup milk
1 cup water
salt and pepper
1 tablespoon sugar
kneaded butter, made with 2 tablespoons butter and 1 tablespoon flour

Method

In a saucepan heat the milk and water, add seasoning to taste and the sugar. Add carrots, cover and simmer 15–20 minutes or until just tender.

Pour off half the cooking liquid and thicken the remainder by adding kneaded butter, a little at a time, shaking the pan and heating until the sauce thickens.

Add the cream and dill, adjust the seasoning, heat well and serve.

Throughout the north of Central Europe **sour cream** is an invaluable ingredient in sauces, but further south, **yogurt** is more often used.

Vegetables in Central Europe are seldom if ever merely boiled or steamed. They are often served in sauces thickened with sweet or sour cream.

Duck with Red Cabbage

4–5 lb duck
1 small red cabbage
salt and pepper
1 apple, quartered and cored
1 orange, peeled and sectioned
3 tablespoons oil
2 tablespoons lemon juice
4 slices of bacon, diced
1 medium onion, coarsely chopped
½ tablespoon flour
1 cup dry red wine
1 bay leaf
1 teaspoon sugar

For garnish
2 apples
2 small oranges

Trussing needle and string

Ducks and geese are common on the Central European dinner table. Here duck is combined with the ubiquitous cabbage.

Method

Set the oven at moderately hot (375°F).

Wipe the inside of the duck with a damp cloth. Season inside the bird with salt and pepper. Stuff the apple quarters and orange sections into the duck cavity. Truss the bird.

In a roasting pan heat the oil, add the duck and baste well with the oil. Prick the skin of the duck to release excess fat, place the duck on a rack and roast in heated oven for 45 minutes or until the duck is brown.

Shred the cabbage, discarding the core, season with salt and sprinkle with lemon juice to help preserve the color.

In a large heavy flameproof casserole fry the bacon over medium heat until brown. Add the onion and cook until soft. Stir in the flour, add the wine, cabbage, bay leaf, sugar and salt and pepper to taste. Stir well. Cover and simmer 10–15 minutes.

Set the browned duck on top of the cabbage, cover and continue cooking over low heat on top of the stove or in a moderate oven (350°F) for 1 hour or until the duck is very tender.

To prepare the garnish: pare, quarter and core the apples; peel and section the oranges and add them both to the casserole 15 minutes before the end of cooking.

Take the duck from the casserole and remove the trussing strings. Arrange the cabbage on a platter, discarding the bay leaf, and place the duck on top; garnish with apple quarters and orange sections.

Roast duck with red cabbage is garnished with quarters of apple and sections of orange

Veal Paprika

2 lb veal breast or shoulder, cut into 1½ inch cubes
1 tablespoon sweet red paprika
2 tablespoons lard or bacon fat
1 medium onion, chopped
salt
¾ cup veal or beef stock
1 tablespoon flour
1 cup sour cream (optional)

True veal paprika does not use sour cream, but this addition gives more sauce.

Method

In a skillet heat the lard or bacon fat and cook the onion until it starts to brown. Toss the veal cubes in paprika to coat them and brown on all sides over medium heat.

Add a little salt and 2 tablespoons stock, cover the pan and cook over very low heat or in a moderately low oven (325°F) for 1 hour or until the veal is tender. If the pan looks dry during cooking, add a little more stock.

Stir in the flour and cook 1 minute. Add the remaining stock and stir until the sauce thickens – it should be a rich red-gold color. Taste it for seasoning.

If you like, just before serving stir in the sour cream and heat the sauce thoroughly without boiling.

Paprika

The Turks introduced paprika to Central Europe but today the spice is typically Hungarian. The world's finest paprika, with a mildly pungent, sweet flavor, is ground from the pods of red bonnet peppers in Hungary.

The strong, hot kind, known as king paprika, is prepared by grinding the seeds, stalks and the pods of the peppers.

Paprika is essential in preparing goulash and gives its name to the popular recipe – veal or chicken paprika. Use sweet red Hungarian paprika for these dishes to be worthy of their reputation.

Lamb with Yogurt

1½–2 lb lamb shoulder, boned and cut in cubes
1 cup plain yogurt
¼ cup oil
3 medium onions, coarsely chopped
salt and pepper
½ cup water
1 cup (½ lb) dried lima beans, soaked for 8 hours and drained
½ cup beef stock or water
4 cloves of garlic, crushed
kneaded butter, made with 2 tablespoons butter and 1 tablespoon flour

Method

In a flameproof casserole heat the oil, add the onions and cook gently until they are soft. Take them out with a slotted spoon, add the cubes of meat to the pot and brown them on all sides.

Put back the onions, season and add ½ cup water. Cover the pot tightly and cook over low heat for ¾–1 hour, stirring from time to time. Add the soaked, drained lima beans with enough water just to cover, replace the lid and cook 30–40 minutes longer or until meat and beans are very tender. If pan gets dry, add more water during cooking.

Add the stock or water and garlic. Bring just back to a boil, add the kneaded butter, a small piece at a time, and cook, shaking the pot gently, until the mixture thickens; adjust the seasoning.

Just before serving, add the yogurt; heat but do not boil.

Czech Torte

2 cups flour
½ teaspoon salt
¼ cup butter
½ cup sugar
1 tablespoon honey, mixed with 1 tablespoon water
1 egg, beaten to mix
1 teaspoon vanilla

For filling
2 squares (2 oz) unsweetened chocolate, cut in pieces
½ cup sugar
1¼ cups milk
4 egg yolks
1½ tablespoons cornstarch
1 cup unsalted butter, softened

To finish
¼ cup browned hazelnuts, finely chopped
¼ cup browned whole hazelnuts

Two 8 inch round cake pans

Central European cakes and dessert pancakes are often prepared in layers with flavored fillings. Serves 6–8.

Method

Set oven at moderate (350°F).

To make the torte: sift the flour with the salt into a bowl. Rub in the butter with the fingertips until the mixture resembles crumbs. Make a well in the center and add the sugar, honey and water mixture, beaten egg and vanilla. With a knife draw the flour into the mixture quickly, adding more water if necessary, to make a smooth dough.

Turn the pastry dough out onto a floured board and knead lightly for about 1 minute. Divide into 6 parts.

Invert the cake pans and grease and flour the bottoms.

Put a portion of the dough on the bottom of each pan and roll with a rolling pin until the dough is thin and covers the entire surface. Bake in the heated oven for 10 minutes or until the pastry circles are golden brown. Cool them slightly before carefully removing from the pans with a metal spatula. Cool on a wire rack.

Continue rolling and baking circles until all are baked.

To make the filling: heat the chocolate and sugar with the milk, stirring until dissolved. Beat the egg yolks and cornstarch until slightly thick, stir in the hot milk mixture and return to the pan. Cook over low heat, stirring constantly, until the custard thickens; simmer 2 minutes. Take from the heat and cool, stirring occasionally. When cold, beat in the softened butter to make a smooth cream.

Spread each circle of pastry with some of the filling and stack the circles on top of each other. Spread the top with the remaining filling, sprinkle with chopped hazelnuts and circle the edge with whole hazelnuts.

Refrigerate the torte overnight to let it mellow. Cut the torte into wedges to serve.

Czech torte – six layers of pastry covered with chocolate filling – is topped with a border of whole hazelnuts

Basic Strudel Dough

1 1/2–2 cups flour
pinch of salt
1 small egg
2 teaspoons oil
1/2 cup warm water

Strudel is a challenge; patience and practice are necessary to perfect spreading and rolling the elastic dough properly, but the melting flakes of good strudel pastry are ample reward for the extra effort. Strudel may have savory or sweet fillings.

Method

Sift the flour into a bowl with the salt and make a well in the center. Beat the egg, add oil and warm water and pour into the well. Work together to make a smooth elastic dough, adding more flour if necessary, so the strudel dough is soft but not sticky.

Knead 5 minutes on a floured board, cover with an inverted bowl and leave in a warm place for 10–15 minutes.

Roll out the dough to 1/4 inch thickness; lift onto a large floured cloth, spread out on a table. (Cloth and table should be at least 3 feet square.) Leave 7–10 minutes for the dough to lose its elasticity.

Stretch the dough very gently, pulling the edges with both hands until it is paper thin and transparent – it is easier for 2 people to do this. If you are alone, hold one side down with a rolling pin while pulling the other.

Spread the dough with the chosen filling and roll up, using the cloth as a guide; bake as directed in recipe.

Note: the following fillings will each fill a 1 1/2–2 cup quantity of strudel dough.

Fillings for Strudel

Poppyseed

3 cups poppyseeds, crushed or ground
1/2 cup milk
1/2 cup sugar
1/2 cup apricot jam
1/2 cup raisins
grated rind of 1/2 lemon
3 tablespoons melted butter

Method

Put poppyseed in a saucepan with milk and sugar, bring to a boil, stirring, then simmer 10 minutes. Take from heat and stir in apricot jam, raisins and lemon rind. Let cool.

Set oven at moderate (350°F) and grease a baking sheet.

Brush the thin sheet of strudel dough with half the melted butter and spread poppyseed mixture evenly on it; trim the edges of the dough.

Roll up the dough carefully, trim the loose edges and tuck in the ends of the roll. Transfer to the baking sheet.

Brush the top with remaining melted butter and bake in heated oven for 30 minutes. Turn oven to hot (400°F) and bake 10 minutes longer or until pastry is crisp and lightly browned. Cut in slices to serve hot or cold.

Apple

2 lb apples, pared, cored and sliced
6 tablespoons melted butter
1/2 cup fresh white breadcrumbs
1/2 cup raisins
1 teaspoon ground cinnamon
1/2 cup sugar
1/4 cup whole blanched almonds, chopped
confectioners' sugar (for sprinkling)

Method

Brush 2 tablespoons butter over the thin sheet of strudel dough. Brown the breadcrumbs in 2 more tablespoons butter. Take from heat and mix in the apple slices, raisins and cinnamon. Spread apple mixture on dough and sprinkle evenly with the 1/2 cup of sugar and chopped almonds. Trim edges of dough.

Set oven at moderate (350°F) and grease a baking sheet.

Roll up the dough carefully, trim the loose edges and tuck in the ends of the roll. Transfer to the baking sheet. Brush the top with remaining melted butter, and bake in heated oven for 30 minutes. Turn oven up to hot (400°F) and bake 10 minutes longer or until pastry is crisp and lightly browned. Dust with confectioners' sugar before cutting into slices and serving hot or cold.

Cream Cheese

1 1/2 cups cream cheese
1/4 cup butter
1/4 cup sugar
1/2 cup dark or golden raisins, soaked in warm water until puffed
grated rind of 1 lemon, and juice of 1/2 lemon
2 teaspoons flour
2 egg yolks or 1 egg, beaten to mix
1/4 cup melted butter
2–3 tablespoons browned breadcrumbs
confectioners' sugar (for sprinkling)

Method

Cream the butter, beat in the sugar until light and fluffy and gradually beat in the cream cheese. Drain raisins and add them to the cheese mixture with the lemon rind and juice, the flour and egg.

Brush the strudel dough carefully with melted butter and scatter with browned breadcrumbs. Dot with the filling and trim loose edges of dough. Roll up strudel carefully, tip it onto a greased baking sheet and form it into a horseshoe. Brush with melted butter and bake in heated oven for 30–40 minutes or until golden brown. Cool, sprinkle with confectioners' sugar, if you like, and cut into slices.

Cabbage

1 medium green cabbage, shredded
2 tablespoons bacon fat
salt and pepper
3 tablespoons melted butter
1/4 cup sour cream
1/2 cup cooked ham, chopped (optional)

Method

In a saucepan melt the bacon fat. Add the cabbage and season to taste. Cook, covered, over low heat, stirring occasionally, for 20–25 minutes or until tender. Set oven at moderately hot (375°F).

Brush strudel dough with a little melted butter, then dot with sour cream. Spread the cabbage evenly over the surface and sprinkle with chopped ham, if used. Trim edges of dough. Lift one edge of the cloth until dough rolls over onto itself. Continue until a long roll is made. Grease a baking sheet.

Trim the loose edges of the dough and tuck in the ends of the roll, shape into a horseshoe and transfer to the baking sheet. Brush the top with remaining melted butter, and bake in heated oven for 35–40 minutes or until the pastry is crisp and lightly browned. Cut in slices to serve hot or cold.

Central European cooking

Cream cheese strudel is baked in a horseshoe-shape and cut in slices to serve

Leek and cheese quiche can be served hot or cold (recipe is on page 118)

IDEAS FOR BRUNCH

Breakfast is too good a meal to miss, and since hearty breakfasts are too early in the day for entertaining, brunch has taken their place. Spicy sausages, crisp bacon and eggs any style are obvious breakfast choices, but brunch has also inspired the revival of half-forgotten favorites like French toast and spoon bread. Here is an excuse to indulge in pancakes, fresh biscuits, muffins, coffeecakes and all the old-fashioned breads that are so good with steaming hot coffee.

But brunch possibilities are not limited by breakfast. The later hour calls for more substantial dishes like ham rarebit that can hold their own with a brisk bloody Mary or a vodka bullshot. Desserts can include fresh fruit cakes and fruit marinated in liqueur as well as the more usual breakfast alternatives of sliced melon, grapefruit, sugared berries or fruit compote.

Brunch is an informal occasion and the food should be informal too. This is an ideal opportunity for a host to demonstrate his skill with the chafing dish, cooking in front of guests so the food goes straight from pan to plate. A chafing dish solves one of the main problems of brunch – many of the most popular dishes like scrambled eggs must be eaten at once. This is easy enough for a few people but if you are choosing a menu for large numbers, look for dishes that can be prepared ahead – omelet for eighteen is the cook's nightmare.

Egg Dishes

Eggs excel at brunch. Light and quick to cook, they go as well in traditional breakfast foods like omelets as they do in off-beat combinations like baked eggs with smoked salmon, and leek quiche.

Eggs have only one disadvantage – they overcook easily so many egg dishes must be served as soon as they are ready.

Eggs en Cocotte with Smoked Salmon

8 eggs
$\frac{1}{4}$ lb smoked salmon, cut in strips
juice of 1 lemon
1 cup heavy cream
salt and pepper
$\frac{1}{2}$ cup grated Gruyère cheese

8 individual cocottes or ramekins

Method

Butter the cocottes or ramekins.

Arrange the salmon in the bottom of the buttered dishes, squeeze over the lemon juice and pour in half the cream.

Break the eggs on top, spoon over the remaining cream, sprinkle with seasoning and then Gruyère cheese.

Stand the cocottes or ramekins in a water bath of very hot water and bake in a moderate oven (350°F) for 10 minutes. Serve at once.

Leek and Cheese Quiche

For rich pie pastry
$1\frac{1}{2}$ cups flour
pinch of salt
6 tablespoons butter
2 tablespoons shortening
2 tablespoons cold water

For filling
2 eggs
2 egg yolks
$\frac{1}{4}$ cup grated Gruyère cheese
$1\frac{1}{2}$ cups light cream or milk
salt and pepper
2 tablespoons butter
white part of 5 medium leeks, thinly sliced

9 inch square flan ring or 10 inch round quiche pan

A substitute for the square flan ring can be made by folding heavy duty foil into a narrow band, then shaping it into a square and fastening with a paper clip.

Method

Make the pastry dough and chill 30 minutes; roll it out and line the flan ring or quiche pan. Set the oven at moderately hot (375°F).

Beat the eggs and egg yolks in a bowl until mixed and stir in the cheese and cream or milk with seasoning to taste.

Melt the butter in a heavy-based pan, add the sliced leeks, press a piece of buttered foil on top and add the lid. Sweat (cook gently) for 12–15 minutes until the leeks are soft but not browned.

Spread the leeks in the pastry shell, pour in the cheese mixture and bake in the heated oven for 25–30 minutes or until the quiche is set and browned.

Watchpoint: do not overcook or it will curdle.

Serve the quiche hot or cool (not chilled).

Plain Omelet

4 eggs
$1\frac{1}{2}$ tablespoons cold water
salt
black pepper, freshly ground
2 tablespoons butter

7–8 inch omelet pan

This quantity makes an omelet for 2. Do not try to make a larger omelet but instead make 2 omelets for 4 people.

Method

Break the eggs into a bowl and beat well with a fork. When the yolks and whites are broken up, add the water and seasoning (this should be done just before cooking).

Heat the pan over medium heat, add the butter in 2 pieces and, as soon as it is foaming, pour in the egg mixture. Leave 10–15 seconds before stirring the egg mixture around slowly with the flat of a fork. Stir once or twice around the pan, then cook for another 5–6 seconds.

Lift up the edge of the omelet to let any remaining raw egg run onto the hot pan. (Some people like omelets to be soft in the center, others prefer them cooked until firm, so the length of cooking time depends on your preference.)

Tilt the pan away from you and fold the omelet over to the far side. Change your grip on the pan so the handle runs up the palm of your hand. Tip the omelet onto a warmed plate, so it is folded in three.

Swiss Omelet

In a small pan fry $\frac{1}{2}$ cup diced ham in 1 tablespoon butter until browned.

Make a plain 4-egg omelet and just before folding it, scatter over the ham and 2–3 tablespoons grated or finely diced Gruyère cheese.

Fold the omelet onto a plate and sprinkle with 1 tablespoon more grated Gruyère cheese before serving.

Sour Cream and Chives Omelet

Make a plain 4-egg omelet but before adding the egg mixture to the pan, stir in 2 tablespoons chopped chives. Spoon $\frac{1}{2}$ cup sour cream into the omelet before folding.

A few spoons of red or black caviar are an excellent addition with the sour cream.

Swiss omelet, filled with diced ham, is sprinkled with grated Gruyère cheese for serving

Mexican baked eggs are set on a mixture flavored with creamed corn, chili, tomatoes and onions

Omelet Clamart

In a small pan melt 1 tablespoon butter, add 2 finely chopped shallots and sauté until soft. Add 1 cup cooked green peas and heat well; stir in 1 tablespoon chopped parsley.

Make a plain 4-egg omelet and just before folding it, scatter over the pea mixture.

Omelet Alsacienne

In a skillet fry 2 slices of diced bacon until crisp. Add $\frac{3}{4}$ cup thinly sliced Strasbourg or frankfurter sausages and cook gently until hot. Add $\frac{2}{3}$ cup cooked sauerkraut and heat thoroughly.

Make a plain 4-egg omelet. Just before folding it, spread over the sauerkraut mixture.

Omelet Lyonnaise

In a saucepan melt 1 tablespoon butter, add 1 finely sliced Bermuda or other mild onion, season, press a piece of foil on top and cook slowly (sweat) for 8–10 minutes or until soft but not browned.

Make a plain 4-egg omelet and just before folding it spread over the onion mixture. Fold omelet onto a plate and keep warm.

In the omelet pan melt 2 tablespoons butter and cook until golden brown. At once add the juice of $\frac{1}{2}$ lemon and 2 teaspoons chopped parsley, mix and pour over the omelet.

Omelet Provençale

This omelet is made with leftover ratatouille (see Volume 6). Heat $1\frac{1}{2}$ cups ratatouille.

Make a plain 4-egg omelet and as soon as the eggs are added to the pan, stir in the ratatouille. Cook until the omelet is almost set on top. Fold or serve flat, as you like.

Mexican Baked Eggs

4–8 eggs (1–2 per person)
2 tablespoons bacon drippings or oil
2 onions, chopped
3 tomatoes, peeled, seeded and chopped
1 fresh or canned serrano or jalapeño chili
2 cloves of garlic, crushed
salt and pepper
3 cups fresh or canned creamed corn
2 tablespoons chopped parsley

Method

If using fresh chili, soak it in water for 1 hour, then drain and chop, discarding the seeds.

Watchpoint: handle fresh chilis wearing gloves to avoid burning the skin. Drain, rinse and chop canned chilis.

In a shallow flameproof casserole or skillet heat the drippings or oil and fry the onion until soft. Add the tomatoes, chili, garlic and salt and pepper and cook, stirring, until the tomatoes and chili are soft. Stir in the corn, heat thoroughly, and taste for seasoning.

Make hollows in the mixture and drop an egg into each. Bake in a moderate oven (350°F) for 6 minutes or until the eggs are just set. Sprinkle chopped parsley around the edge of the dish just before serving.

Costa Rican Onion Pie

For pastry
2 cups flour
$\frac{1}{2}$ teaspoon salt
2 teaspoons baking powder
1 tablespoon shortening
1 tablespoon butter
1 egg
$\frac{3}{4}$ cup sour cream

For filling
4 large Bermuda or other mild onions, thinly sliced
2 tablespoons butter
salt and pepper
1 egg, separated
$1\frac{1}{2}$ cups sour cream

9 inch flan ring or pie pan with removable base

Method

To make the pastry dough: sift the flour with the salt and baking powder into a bowl, rub in the shortening and butter with fingertips and make a well in the center. Beat the egg with the sour cream, pour into the well and stir in the flour. Knead lightly to form a smooth dough and chill 30 minutes.

To make the filling: in a heavy-based pan melt 2 tablespoons butter, add the onions and seasoning, press a piece of buttered foil on top and add the lid. Cook gently (sweat) for 20 minutes or until the onions are very soft, stirring occasionally. Remove the lid and foil and cook until any liquid has evaporated.

Stiffly beat the egg white, fold it into the yolk and stir this mixture into the onions with the sour cream. Cook gently, stirring, until the mixture thickens slightly, but do not let it boil. Taste for seasoning and cool.

Set oven at hot (400°F). Line the flan ring or pie pan with two-thirds of the dough and add the filling.

Roll out the remaining dough to cover the pie, lay it on top of the pie and seal the pastry edges by fluting with the finger and thumb. Make 2 slits in the center with scissors for steam to escape and chill 15 minutes.

Bake the pie in the heated oven for 10 minutes, lower temperature to moderate (350°F) and continue baking 25 minutes or until pastry is browned. Serve hot or cold.

Shrimp casserole Florentine is sprinkled with grated nutmeg and pepper before serving

Fish and Meat Dishes

Fish such as kippers and finnan haddie, together with meats like kidneys, have long been part of the traditional English breakfast and they are equally good for brunch. Most of the following suggestions can be prepared in advance.

Shrimp Casserole Florentine

1½ lb cooked, peeled shrimps
1½ lb fresh or 2 packages frozen spinach
¼ cup butter
béchamel sauce, made with
3 tablespoons butter,
3 tablespoons flour and
2 cups milk (infused with slice of onion, bay leaf, blade of mace and 6 peppercorns)
¼ cup grated Gruyère cheese
pinch of grated nutmeg
salt and pepper

Method

Wash the fresh spinach thoroughly and cook it in boiling salted water for 5 minutes or until tender; cook frozen spinach according to package directions. Drain the spinach, press it dry between 2 plates and chop it.

Melt half the butter in a pan and sauté the spinach 2–3 minutes until dry. Season and spread the spinach in the bottom of a baking dish. Spread two-thirds of the shrimps on top and coat with the béchamel sauce; sprinkle over the grated Gruyère cheese.

Bake the casserole in a moderate oven (350°F) for 15–20 minutes or until very hot and browned.

Melt the remaining butter and sauté the remaining shrimps until very hot. Sprinkle with nutmeg and a little pepper and arrange them around the edge of the dish.

Potted Salmon

1¼–1½ lb fresh salmon steaks
½ cup white wine
salt and pepper
1 teaspoon anchovy paste
¼ teaspoon ground mace
pinch of cayenne
1 cup melted butter
⅓ cup clarified butter

Method

Put the salmon steaks in a baking dish, pour over the wine and sprinkle with salt and pepper. Cover with buttered foil and bake in a moderate oven (350°F) for 15 minutes or until the fish flakes easily. Cool, then drain the salmon and flake it, discarding the bones.

Mix the salmon with the anchovy paste, mace, cayenne and melted butter and purée the mixture, a little at a time, in a blender. Beat the purée so it is thoroughly mixed and taste for seasoning.

Pack the salmon mixture into a crock, making sure all air is excluded, and pour a layer of melted clarified butter on top.

Keep potted salmon in the refrigerator for at least 3 days and up to 2 weeks before serving with wholewheat crackers or hot toast.

Potted fish and meats were developed in the days before refrigeration as a way of keeping perishable ingredients for relatively long periods. Potted meats were particularly popular on long sea voyages.

The ingredients are puréed, mixed with spices and packed into a crock with a layer of butter or fat on top to exclude all the air.

Fish Pie

3 cups (1¼ lb) cooked flaked white fish, preferably cod or haddock
béchamel sauce, made with
5 tablespoons butter,
5 tablespoons flour and
3 cups milk (infused with bay leaf, 6 peppercorns, blade of mace and slice of onion)
3 hard-cooked eggs, sliced
3 tomatoes, peeled and sliced
salt and pepper
mashed potatoes, made with
4 medium potatoes,
3–4 tablespoons butter,
½ cup milk and salt and pepper

Method

Spread half the fish in a buttered baking dish and spoon over a little béchamel sauce. Cover with the sliced eggs, then with the sliced tomatoes, sprinkle with seasoning and coat with some of the béchamel sauce. Add the remaining fish and sauce and coat the dish completely with mashed potatoes.

Bake the fish pie in a moderate oven (350°F) for 20–30 minutes or until the potatoes are browned and the sauce begins to bubble up around the sides of the dish.

Fisherman's Oyster Stew

$1\frac{1}{2}$ pints shucked oysters, with their liquor
$\frac{1}{4}$ lb piece of bacon, diced
1 large onion, chopped
3 stalks of celery, chopped
2 tomatoes, peeled, seeded and chopped
3 cups water
1 teaspoon oregano
1 cup pasta shells, uncooked
$\frac{1}{4}$ teaspoon crushed dried red pepper
salt and pepper
$\frac{1}{4}$ cup chopped parsley
oyster crackers (for serving)

Method

In a large saucepan fry the bacon until browned. Add the onion and celery and cook gently until they begin to brown.

Strain the oysters, reserve them and add the liquor to the pan with the tomatoes, water, oregano, pasta shells, red pepper and seasoning. Cover, bring to a boil and simmer 10 minutes or until the pasta shells are tender.

Add the reserved oysters and chopped parsley and simmer 2 minutes longer or until the edges of the oysters curl. Taste for seasoning and serve at once in bowls with oyster crackers.

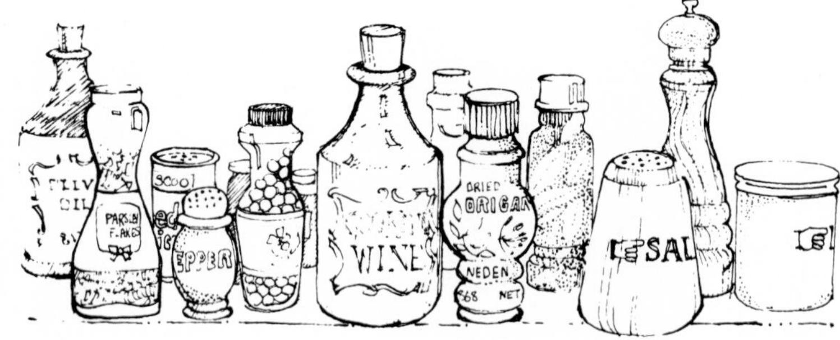

Shrimp and Orange Salad

$\frac{1}{2}$ lb cooked peeled shrimps, chopped
4 large oranges
2 medium carrots, grated
1 hard-cooked egg (for garnish)

For lemon dressing
$1\frac{1}{2}$ tablespoons lemon juice
3 tablespoons oil
3 tablespoons light cream
$\frac{1}{2}$ teaspoon salt
2 teaspoons sugar
black pepper, freshly ground

Method

Cut the tops off the oranges and scoop out the flesh as neatly as possible with a teaspoon. Cut between the skin of the oranges to loosen the sections and mix the flesh with the shrimps and carrots.

To make the lemon dressing: beat all the ingredients together and taste for seasoning.

Mix the dressing with the shrimp mixture and pile it into the orange shells. Separate the egg yolk and white, finely chop the white and sprinkle it around the edge of the oranges. Work the egg yolk through a strainer to decorate the middle of the oranges. Chill before serving.

Ham Rarebit

$\frac{1}{2}$ lb (about $1\frac{1}{2}$ cups) cooked ham, ground or finely chopped
3 tablespoons butter
1 onion, chopped
1 cup ($\frac{1}{4}$ lb) mushrooms, chopped
1 tablespoon flour
1 cup heavy cream
1 teaspoon tarragon
salt and pepper
4 thick slices of white bread, toasted, or 2 English muffins, split and toasted
4 slices of Gruyère cheese, halved crosswise
bunch of watercress (for garnish)

4 individual gratin or baking dishes

Method

In a saucepan melt the butter and fry the onion until soft but not browned. Add the mushrooms and cook until soft. Stir in the flour, pour in the cream and bring to a boil, stirring until the sauce thickens. Add the ham, tarragon and seasoning.

Place the toasted bread or English muffins in the dishes and spread with the ham mixture. Top each with 2 slices of Gruyère cheese and bake in a moderately hot oven (375°F) for 15 minutes or until browned. Garnish each dish with watercress before serving.

Deviled Kidneys

8 lamb kidneys

For devil sauce
$\frac{1}{2}$ cup butter
1 teaspoon salt
1 tablespoon dark brown sugar
$\frac{1}{2}$ teaspoon black pepper, freshly ground
$\frac{1}{2}$ teaspoon dry mustard
$\frac{1}{2}$ teaspoon ground ginger
2 teaspoons Worcestershire sauce
1 teaspoon soy sauce

For serving
1 tablespoon chopped parsley
crisp bacon

4 kebab skewers

Method

To make the devil sauce: in a small pan melt the butter, add the remaining devil sauce ingredients and cook gently for 2 minutes.

Remove the skins from the kidneys (if not already done) and cut out the core with scissors. Cut the kidneys almost in half, leaving them joined at one side, and open them flat to 'butterfly' them.

Thread the kidneys flat on the skewers, allowing 2 kidneys to each skewer. Brush the kidneys with the devil sauce and broil them 2–3 inches from the flame, allowing 2–3 minutes on each side for rare kidneys. Baste them often with the devil sauce during broiling.

To serve, arrange the kidneys on a platter, sprinkle with chopped parsley, garnish the dish with crisp slices of bacon and serve at once.

Ham rarebit is baked on toasted bread or English muffins and garnished with watercress

Corn cakes are cooked on a griddle or skillet; serve them with butter and preserves

Breads, Biscuits and Pancakes

No brunch is complete without a good selection of breads and biscuits. Here are some old favorites and one or two new suggestions.

Corn Cakes

1½ cups yellow corn meal
¾ cup sugar
½ cup oil
2 eggs, beaten to mix
1½ cups flour
3 teaspoons baking powder
pinch of salt
1 cup milk
piece of fat bacon (for greasing)

Griddle or heavy skillet

Makes 20–22 cakes.

Method

Beat the sugar with the oil for about 5 minutes. Beat in the eggs, Sift the flour with the baking powder and salt and stir in the corn meal. Stir the corn meal mixture into the egg mixture alternately with the milk and let batter stand about 30 minutes.

Rub the bacon over a griddle or heavy skillet to grease it thoroughly. To test if it is ready, heat it until a little water dripped on the surface bounces back.

Pour the batter into even cakes and cook until bubbles appear on the surface and the underside is brown. Turn the cakes and brown the other side.

Pile the corn cakes one on top of another, with a paper towel between each to absorb steam. Cook the remaining cakes in the same way, greasing the griddle when necessary. Serve as soon as possible with butter and preserves.

French Toast

8 slices of firm dry white bread, preferably homemade
2 eggs
pinch of salt
⅔ cup of milk
½ teaspoon vanilla
4–6 tablespoons butter
maple syrup or 2 teaspoons cinnamon, mixed with ¼ cup sugar (for serving)

Method

Beat the eggs until well mixed and stir in the salt, milk and vanilla. Dip half the slices of bread in the egg mixture, turning them so they are soaked on both sides.

Heat half the butter in a skillet and fry the soaked bread until browned, turn and brown on the other side. Keep the slices hot while soaking and frying the remaining bread in the same way.

Serve the toast with maple syrup or cinnamon sugar.

Corn Dollars

1 cup fresh or canned creamed corn
2 eggs, separated
¼ cup flour
1 teaspoon baking powder
½ teaspoon salt
¼ teaspoon pepper
¼ cup milk
4–5 tablespoons butter
crisply fried slices of bacon (for serving)

Method

Beat the corn until it is light and beat in the egg yolks. Stir in the flour, baking powder, salt and pepper, then the milk. Stiffly whip the egg whites and fold into the mixture.

In a skillet melt half the butter and, when foaming, drop in tablespoons of the corn mixture to make rounds the size of a silver dollar. Fry the rounds until golden, turn them and brown the other sides.

Arrange the corn dollars, overlapping, on a platter and keep warm while frying the remaining mixture. Serve them as soon as possible with crisply fried bacon.

Molasses Bread

½ cup molasses
2 cups all-purpose flour
1 package dry yeast or 1 cake compressed yeast
1 cup lukewarm milk
1½ teaspoons salt
2 cups wholewheat flour
1 egg, beaten to mix with ½ teaspoon salt (for glaze)

Large loaf pan (9 X 5 X 3 inches)

Method

Sprinkle or crumble the yeast over the milk and let stand 5 minutes or until dissolved.

Sift the all-purpose flour into a bowl with the salt, stir in the wholewheat flour and make a well in the center. Add the yeast mixture and molasses and stir with the hand to form a dough that is soft but not sticky.

Turn out the dough onto a lightly floured board and knead 5 minutes or until the dough is smooth and elastic. Put it in a lightly oiled bowl, cover with a damp cloth and let rise in a warm place for 1½ hours or until it is doubled in bulk.

Set oven at moderately hot (375°F) and grease the loaf pan.

Knead the dough lightly to knock out the air, shape it and put in the prepared loaf pan. Let dough rise again in a warm place for 30 minutes or until almost doubled in bulk. Brush with egg glaze and bake in the heated oven for 40 minutes or until the loaf sounds hollow when tapped. Transfer to a wire rack to cool.

Bran Biscuits

1 cup all-bran cereal
2 cups all-purpose flour
$\frac{1}{2}$ teaspoon salt
2 teaspoons baking soda
1 teaspoon cream of tartar
2 tablespoons sugar
$\frac{1}{2}$ cup butter
$\frac{1}{3}$–$\frac{1}{2}$ cup buttermilk

Makes about 12 biscuits.

Method
Set oven at hot (425°F).

Sift the all-purpose flour with the salt, baking soda and cream of tartar into a bowl. Stir in the bran and sugar. Work in the butter with the fingertips until the mixture resembles crumbs.

Make a well in the center, add enough buttermilk to make a soft dough and mix quickly until almost smooth.

Turn the dough onto a floured board, knead lightly, then roll or pat it out to about $\frac{3}{4}$ inch thickness. Cut the dough into 3 inch triangles, transfer to a lightly floured baking sheet and bake in the heated oven for 10–12 minutes or until the biscuits are lightly browned. Serve them at once with butter and honey or preserves.

Ginger Pancakes

1 teaspoon ground ginger
1$\frac{1}{2}$ cups flour
1 teaspoon salt
3 tablespoons sugar
2 teaspoons baking powder
2 eggs, beaten to mix
3 tablespoons melted butter
1$\frac{1}{4}$–1$\frac{1}{2}$ cups milk

Griddle or heavy skillet

Makes 24–26 pancakes (4 inch diameter).

Method
Sift the flour with the salt, sugar, ginger and baking powder into a bowl. Make a well in the center and add the eggs, melted butter and milk. Stir until the batter is almost smooth and let stand at least 1–2 hours.

Lightly grease a griddle or heavy skillet with butter; heat it until a little water dropped on the surface bounces back.

Pour the batter into even cakes onto the griddle or skillet and cook until bubbles appear on the surface and the undersides are browned. Turn and brown the other sides. Pile the pancakes one on top of another, with a paper towel between each to absorb steam.

Serve the pancakes as soon as possible with honey sauce.

Honey Sauce

For 1 cup quantity: heat 1 cup honey until it is melted. Stir in the juice of 1 lemon and serve warm.

Desserts

The fruits you serve fresh for breakfast make excellent desserts for brunch – recipes like grapefruit soufflé give new life to old favorites.

Grapefruit Soufflé

2 grapefruits, halved
confectioners' sugar (for sprinkling)

For soufflé mixture
$\frac{3}{4}$ cup grapefruit marmalade
4 egg whites
$\frac{1}{4}$ cup sugar

The same recipe can be made with oranges and orange marmalade. Allow 1 medium orange per person with the above quantity of soufflé mixture.

Method
To prepare grapefruit: using a grapefruit knife with a curved serrated blade, remove the core, then cut around between the flesh and the pith so the flesh is completely detached from the shell. Slip the knife down each side of the membrane dividing the grapefruit sections, then lift out all the membranes in one piece, leaving the flesh in the grapefruit shell. Discard all seeds.

To make the soufflé: work the marmalade through the strainer into a small saucepan and heat until fairly warm. Stiffly whip the egg whites, then beat in the sugar until the mixture is glossy. Fold one-quarter of this meringue into the warm marmalade, add to the remaining meringue and fold together as lightly as possible.

Pile the soufflé mixture into the grapefruit shells and bake in a hot oven (425°F) for 8–9 minutes or until the soufflés are puffed and brown. Sprinkle with confectioners' sugar and serve at once.

Spiced Bananas

6 bananas, halved lengthwise
$\frac{1}{4}$ cup dark brown sugar
1 teaspoon ground cinnamon
$\frac{1}{2}$ teaspoon ground allspice
$\frac{1}{2}$ teaspoon ground cloves
$\frac{1}{4}$ teaspoon ground cardamom
$\frac{1}{4}$ cup butter

Method
Thickly spread a shallow baking dish with half the butter and put in the bananas.

Mix the sugar with the spices, sprinkle over the bananas and dot with remaining butter. Bake in a moderate oven (350°F) for 20 minutes or until the top is browned.

Serve the bananas with heavy cream or sour cream.

Ideas for brunch

Grapefruit soufflé is an unusual way to serve fresh fruit for brunch

Coeur à la Crème

1 cup creamed cottage cheese
1 cup cream cheese
1 cup heavy cream
pinch of salt

For serving
1 quart strawberries
$\frac{1}{4}$ cup sugar (or to taste)
granulated sugar

Heart-shaped wicker basket

Method
Work the cottage cheese through a strainer and beat with the cream cheese until smooth and light. Gradually beat in the cream and add the salt.

Line a heart-shaped wicker basket with cheesecloth, fill with the cheese mixture, cover and let stand overnight on a plate in the refrigerator for the whey to drain. If no basket is available, let the mixture drain in a colander lined with cheesecloth, then pack into a heart-shaped cake pan.

Select a dozen strawberries for decoration; hull the rest, sprinkle them with sugar, cover and let stand 3–6 hours to draw out the juice.

A short time before serving, unmold the crème onto a platter and surround with whole strawberries. Serve the reserved strawberries in sugar separately. Pass a bowl of granulated sugar for sprinkling.

Coeur à la crème is a French favorite for early summer, timed to coincide with the first fresh strawberries and raspberries. It is a very light form of cream cheese, set in a heart shape in special wicker baskets or china molds with small holes for the whey to drain.

Melon and Strawberry Cup

1 medium cantaloupe or honeydew melon
1 quart strawberries, hulled
$\frac{1}{4}$ cup sugar or to taste
juice of 1 orange
2–3 tablespoons Curaçao, Triple Sec, Grand Marnier or other orange liqueur

Method
Cut the melon in half, discard the seeds and scoop out the flesh with a ball cutter. Scrape the melon shells and cut them in quarters.

Put the melon balls in a bowl with the strawberries, sprinkle with the sugar and pour over the orange juice and liqueur. Cover and chill at least 2 hours or up to 8 hours.

Pile the macerated fruits into the melon shells just before serving.

Blueberry Cake

1 cup fresh or frozen blueberries
$\frac{1}{2}$ cup butter
$\frac{3}{4}$ cup dark brown sugar
2 eggs, beaten to mix
1 teaspoon vanilla
2 cups flour
2 teaspoons baking powder
$\frac{1}{2}$ teaspoon salt
1 cup milk

Large loaf pan (9 X 5 X 3 inches)

Method
Pick over fresh blueberries, wash them and dry thoroughly on paper towels; do not thaw frozen berries.

Grease the loaf pan and set the oven at moderate (350°F).

Cream the butter, gradually add the sugar and beat until soft and fluffy. Beat the eggs into the sugar mixture a little at a time. Continue beating for 2 minutes. Add the vanilla.

Sift the flour with the baking powder and salt and stir into the egg mixture alternately with the milk. Lastly stir in the blueberries and spoon the batter into the prepared pan.

Bake in the heated oven for 60–65 minutes or until a skewer inserted in the center of the cake comes out clean. Transfer to a wire rack to cool.

Chafing Dish Suggestions

Chafing dish recipes are fun – the cook has a chance to show his skill while guests enjoy the performance.

Most chafing dish recipes are simple to make but they are cooked quickly, so it is important to have all the ingredients measured and equipment ready at hand before you begin.

Scrambled Eggs with Chicken Livers

8 eggs
1 cup ($\frac{1}{2}$ lb) chicken livers
$\frac{1}{4}$ cup heavy cream
pinch of ground nutmeg
salt
black pepper, freshly ground
3 tablespoons butter
2 shallots or scallions, finely chopped
1 tablespoon chopped parsley (for sprinkling)
4 slices of white bread, toasted and buttered (for serving)

Chafing dish

Method
Cut the chicken livers in $\frac{1}{2}$ inch slices, discarding any membrane. Beat the eggs until well mixed and stir in the cream, nutmeg and seasoning.

Melt the butter in a chafing dish and sauté the scallions until soft. Add the chicken livers, cook briskly until they are browned, turn them and brown on the other side.

Lower the heat to moderate, add the eggs and cook, stirring, until they begin to thicken. With a wooden spoon, lift large creamy flakes of egg from the bottom of the pan. When almost done to your taste, turn out the heat – the eggs will continue cooking in the heat of the pan.

Sprinkle the scrambled egg mixture with chopped parsley and serve at once on buttered white toast.

Shrimp Wiggle

1½ lb cooked, peeled shrimps
¼ cup butter
3 tablespoons flour
1 cup milk
1 cup light cream
2 cups cooked green peas
salt and pepper

Chafing dish

Method

Melt the butter in the chafing dish, stir in the flour and, when foaming, pour in the milk and cream. Bring to a boil, stirring until the sauce thickens.

Add the shrimps, peas and plenty of seasoning and cook over medium heat until very hot. Serve shrimp wiggle with boiled rice or rice pilaf.

Sweet and Sour Ham

8–10 thin slices of cooked ham
2 tablespoons butter
¼ cup red currant jelly
½ cup sherry
½ teaspoon Tabasco

Chafing dish

Method

In a chafing dish melt the butter, add the red currant jelly and heat gently until it is melted. Stir in the sherry and Tabasco and simmer 1 minute.

Add ham slices, and cook until very hot, basting well with sauce. Serve with creamed spinach (see page 103).

Tongue Dijonnaise

8–10 thin slices of cooked tongue
1–2 tablespoons prepared or Dijon-style mustard
¼ cup oil
2 tablespoons butter
2 teaspoons Worcestershire sauce or to taste
French bread (for serving)

Chafing dish

Method

Spread the slices of tongue on both sides with mustard, then dip them in oil. Pile the slices on top of each other on a plate and set another plate on top to press out any excess oil. Let stand 1–2 hours.

Melt half the butter in the chafing dish, add half the slices of tongue and sprinkle with Worcestershire sauce. Cook briskly, until the slices are browned, turn them and brown on the other side.

Cook the remaining slices of tongue in the same way and serve them with French bread and creamed spinach (see page 103).

Italian Chicken

3–3½ lb cooked chicken, cut in pieces
3 tablespoons olive oil
1 teaspoon paprika
½ teaspoon thyme
½ teaspoon basil
salt and pepper
1 onion, finely chopped
¼ cup brandy
1 cup tomato sauce
1 cup chicken stock

Chafing dish

Method

Heat the olive oil in a chafing dish, add the paprika, herbs and seasoning and put in the pieces of chicken. Turn them so they are well coated with oil and seasonings and sauté them briskly until browned on all sides.

When the chicken pieces are almost brown, add the chopped onion. Pour in the brandy and flame. Add the tomato sauce and stock, cover and simmer 5 minutes.

Taste the sauce for seasoning and serve the chicken with cooked spaghetti or other pasta.

Serve Italian chicken, flamed in brandy, with pasta

Butterscotch Strawberries

1 quart strawberries, hulled

For sauce
1 cup whipping cream
¾ cup dark brown sugar
2–3 tablespoons rum or brandy

Chafing dish

Method

To make the sauce: put the cream in the chafing dish, sprinkle over the sugar and heat, stirring, until the sugar dissolves. Bring to a boil and cook 1 minute.

Add the strawberries, stir in the rum or brandy and heat, basting the strawberries with sauce, until hot. Serve.

Alternatively, the sauce can be kept hot over a low light and guests can dip in the strawberries, speared on forks or toothpicks, as for fondue.

Whiskey Apples

5–6 Golden Delicious or other dessert apples, pared, halved and cored
½ cup sugar
grated rind and juice of ½ lemon
2 inch piece of cinnamon stick
½ cup whiskey

Chafing dish

Method

Put the sugar, lemon rind and juice, cinnamon stick and whiskey in a chafing dish and heat gently until the sugar is dissolved. Add the apples, cover and simmer 10 minutes or until almost tender.

Remove the lid and continue cooking, basting constantly, until the sauce is syrupy and caramelized and the apples are tender. Discard the cinnamon stick before serving.

MEASURING & MEASUREMENTS

The recipe quantities in the Course are measured in standard level teaspoons, tablespoons and cups and their equivalents are shown below. Any liquid pints and quarts also refer to U.S. standard measures.

When measuring dry ingredients, fill the cup or spoon to overflowing without packing down and level the top with a knife. All the dry ingredients, including flour, should be measured before sifting, although sifting may be called for later in the instructions.

Butter and margarine usually come in measured sticks (1 stick equals $\frac{1}{2}$ cup) and other bulk fats can be measured by displacement. For $\frac{1}{3}$ cup fat, fill the measuring cup $\frac{2}{3}$ full of water. Add fat until the water reaches the 1 cup mark. Drain the cup of water and the fat remaining equals $\frac{1}{3}$ cup.

For liquids, fill the measure to the brim, or to the calibration line.

Often quantities of seasonings cannot be stated exactly, for ingredients vary in the amount they require. The instructions 'add to taste' are literal, for it is impossible to achieve just the right balance of flavors in many dishes without tasting them.

Liquid measure	Volume equivalent
3 teaspoons	1 tablespoon
2 tablespoons	1 fluid oz
4 tablespoons	$\frac{1}{4}$ cup
16 tablespoons	1 cup or 8 fluid oz
2 cups	1 pint
2 pints	1 quart
4 quarts	1 gallon

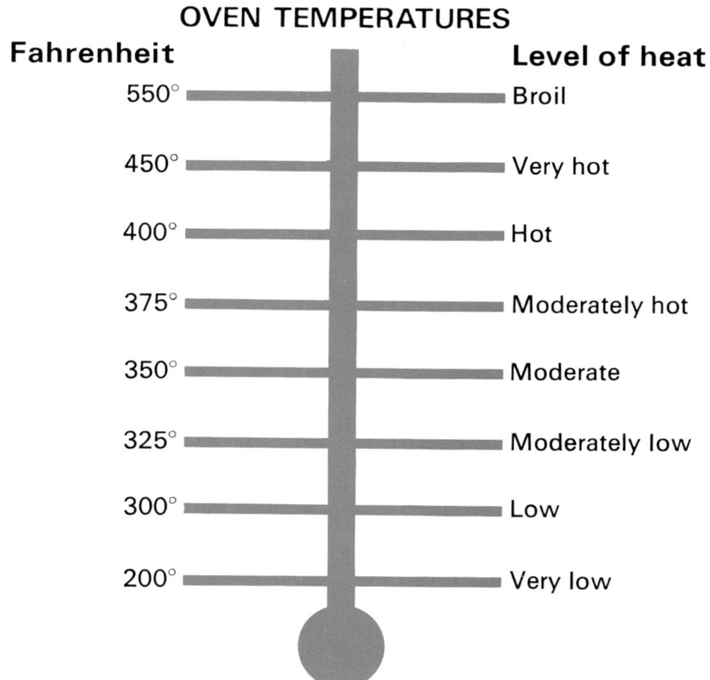

OVEN TEMPERATURES AND SHELF POSITIONS

Throughout the Cooking Course, oven temperatures are stated in degrees Fahrenheit and in generally agreed levels of heat such as 'high' and 'moderate'. The equivalents are shown on the table above.

However, exact temperature varies in different parts of an oven and the thermostat reading refers to the heat in the middle. As the oven temperature at top and bottom can vary as much as 25°F from this setting, the positioning of shelves is very important. In general, heat rises, so the hottest part of the oven is at the top, but consult the manufacturer's handbook about your individual model.

Pans and dishes of food should be placed parallel with burners or elements to avoid scorched edges.

When baking cakes, there must be room for the heat to circulate in the oven around baking sheets and cake pans; otherwise the underside of the cakes will burn. If baking more than one cake in an oven that has back burners or elements, arrange the cakes side by side. If the oven has side burners, arrange cakes back and front.

Oven thermostats are often inaccurate and are unreliable at extremely high or low temperatures. If you do a great deal of baking or question the accuracy of your oven, use a separate oven thermometer as a check on the thermostat.

Cooking Curiosities

A Penchant for Picnics

Since Adam and Eve man has enjoyed eating outside. The inveterate picnicker will spend half the warm months eating out-of-doors despite every inconvenience. The fashion for picnics caused quite a scandal in 1836 when French Impressionist painter Edouard Manet exhibited 'The Picnic'. The scene shows a group of well-dressed men seated on the grass with some women enjoying an al fresco lunch – a conventional enough scene except that one of the women is stark naked!

Open-air feasts are at their best with good wine, fresh bread, and a few cold meats. Mrs. Beeton, the 19th century author of an English book on household management wrote: 'Provided care has been taken in choosing congenial guests, and that in a mixed party one sex does not preponderate, a well-arranged picnic is one of the pleasantest forms of entertainment . . . Avoid serving plenty of salad and no dressing . . . an abundance of wine and no corkscrew.' Sound advice for anyone with a penchant for picnics.

Cooking Curiosities

The Mansell Collection

INDEX

(Volume 10)

A

B

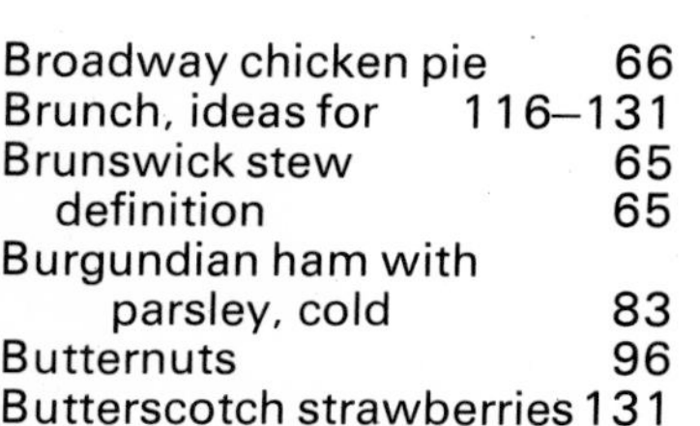

C

Index

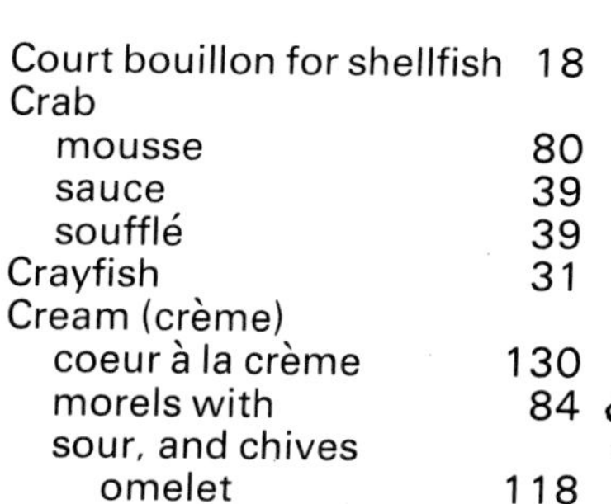

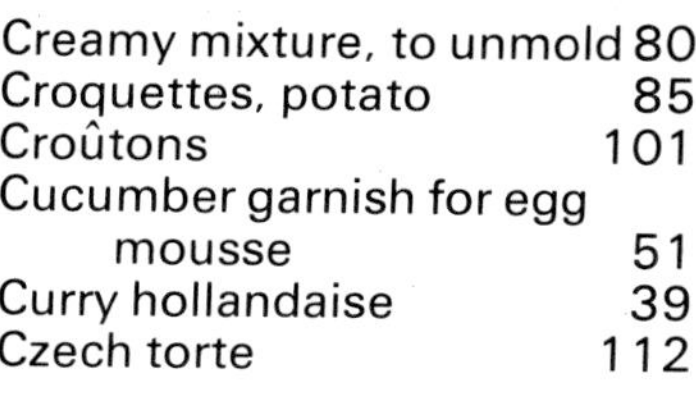

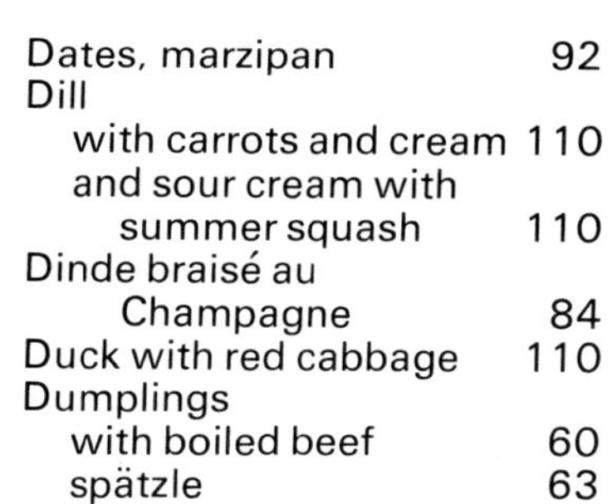

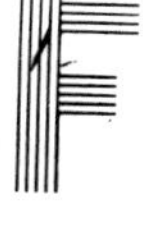

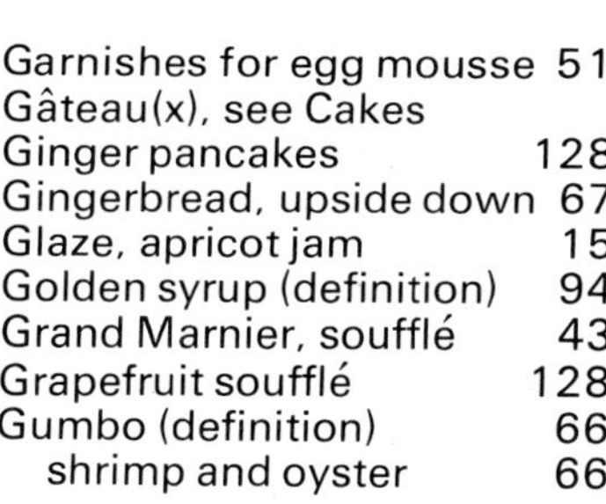

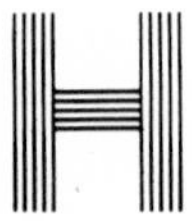

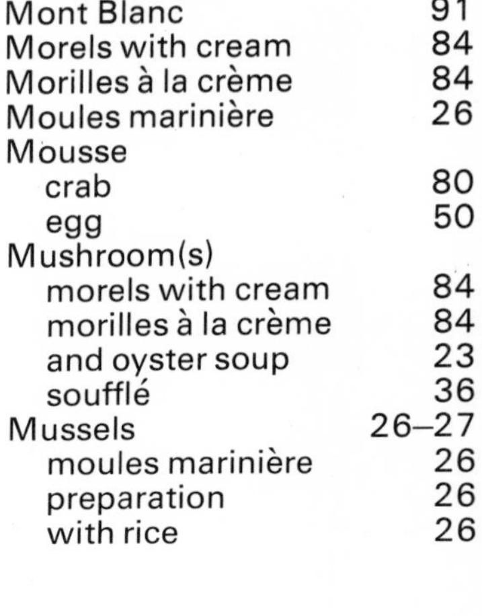

N

Index

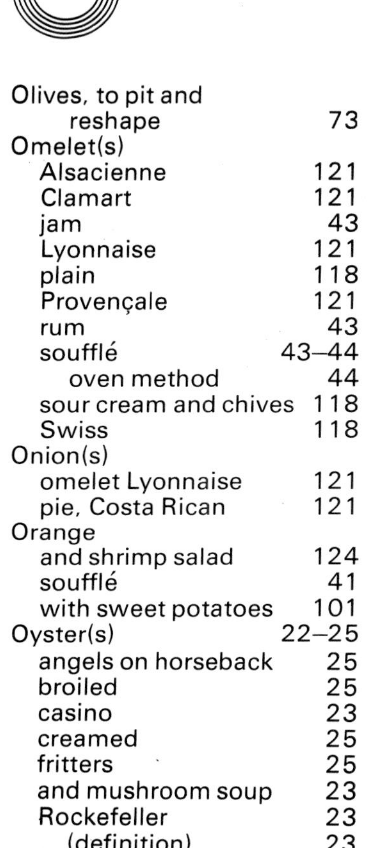

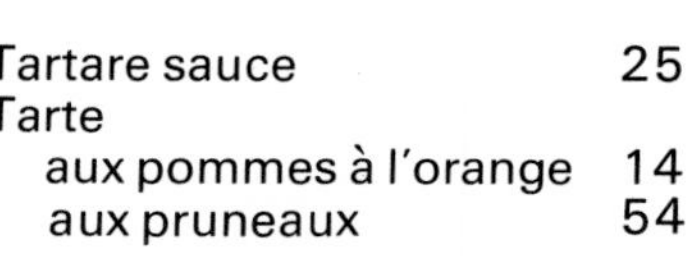

Acknowledgments
Photographs by Fred J. Maroon on pages 13, 16, 22, 85, 93, 106, 109, 111 and 113. Photograph by Ross Chapple on page 131; styling by Fay Abell. Other photographs by Michael Leale, Roger Phillips and John Cowderoy.

Notes